Smile!

Your Key to Inner and Outer Radiance

Elan Sun Star

Roaring Lion Publishing, Inc.
P.O. Box 8492
Asheville, NC 28814
www.roaringlionpublishing.com

Testimonials for *Smile!*

If you saw the film *Apollo 13* about my challenge during the re-entry on the Apollo 13 mission to the moon—you saw how we safely landed the spacecraft, and I can guarantee that I had a giant smile on my face. When the ship picked us up and we emerged from the capsule onto the deck, the whole ship was one big smile!

I can also say that the whole world that was watching anxiously was one big smile when we came through it alive. How could we not smile? Great and good feelings always bring a smile like this. You always get a response with a smile.

"Smile and the world smiles with you" is a powerful and well-known fact. Not a theory. Smiles also open up the door to friendly negotiations in every field where conflict resolution is an issue.

This book *Smile!* can show you why everyone was smiling when we made it back to earth alive and well from Apollo 13 and the moon.

Captain James Lovell, U.S. Navy
Apollo 13 moon landing for NASA

☼

Smile is something we all need to do, and *Smile!* (the book) is something we all need to read. I have seen it work miracles.

Edgar Mitchell, Astronaut
Founder of *Institute of Noetic Sciences*

☼

This book of smile photographs is very uplifting! *Smile!* comes at a time when life is full of pain and anguish. Smiles are good for the heart and for peace.

It is essential for everyone not only to possess a copy but to read it and spread the smiles far and wide around the world.

Arun Gandhi, Founder/President
Mahatma Gandhi Institute for Nonviolence—An organization to strengthen and co-create global peace
Grandson of Mahatma Gandhi

☼

Smile! is a wonderful little book with much to say about a little device—the simple act of smiling. It can literally change one's life over night. We need more information of this kind in our world.

Neale Donald Walsch
Author of *Conversations with God*
Featured in the international hit film, *The Secret*

☼

If you only read one book, read *Smile!*

In my super-active 50 years of training Hollywood's celeb-
rities like Marilyn Monroe; Clark Gable; Errol Flynn; Betty
Grable; Douglas Fairbanks, Jr.; Rita Hayworth; Marlon
Brando; Johnny Weissmuller; Buster Crabbe; Chuck
Norris; Tyrone Power; Matt Dillon; business tycoons like
H.L. Hunt; athletes like Rocky Marciano; astronauts like
James Lovell and Alan Shepard; and thousands of others,
I have seen the power of the human smile to empower
and transform and to bring health and vitality as well
as love and admiration and charisma and even self-
esteem.

All of my world-famous clients were famous because of
their endearing and charismatic smiles...the same smiles
that you possess. *Smile!* is a book you will want share
with others and return to again and again to inspire
yourself and brighten your day and your attitude.

The research in this powerful book is scientific as well as
anecdotal, and it reminds us of the power we hold in the
ability to **smile**.

Dr. Bob Delmonteque, N.D.
Trainer and coach to thousands of Hollywood stars,
CEOs, astronauts and athletes since 1940.
www.bobdelmonteque.com

☼

In a world of technical solutions, converging societies, and globalization, there are still some truisms in humanity that cannot be "spun" or misinterpreted, one of which is the warmth of the human smile.

Amidst the brutality of war in Iraq, the endless attempts to feed starving children in Haiti, the thankless separating of belligerents in Bosnia and Kosovo, or providing humanitarian assistance to Central America, the enduring power of the human smile still spans the barriers of culture, language and hatred.

Elan Sun Star has captured and reminded us of this truism, and I have witnessed his premise at the most basic levels of human endeavor for over 24 years in the United States Army.

Smile! is a must read for those who have lost their ability to smile. It can change our planet.

Colonel **Christopher P. Hughes**
Commander, Joint Task Force Bravo
United States Army, Soto Cano Airbase, Honduras

☼

In my career as a United Nations Command negotiator with North Korea and as the captain of a nuclear submarine in the Persian Gulf during Operation Enduring Freedom on the *USS Pasadena*, I have experienced some of life's most demanding and potentially stressful encounters.

The simple yet profound gesture of a human smile has the innate power to transform extremely stressful situations into more positive and rewarding experiences—even the ones like these.

This book *Smile!* has the information and research and credible comments that are both scientific as well as humane. You will find *Smile!* the book and smiling to be valuable resources for being genuinely happy in your life.

Donald Fritts, U.S. Naval Commander, Ret.
Former United Nations peace negotiator

☼

"Smiling increases your face value." Elan Sun Star's new book, *Smile!*, is a thorough and comprehensive treatment of the important subject of smiling.

The superb photos are uplifting, inspiring, and heart-warming.

The text has been thoroughly researched and is full of common sense, humor, and solid science.

This book needs to be on the coffee table of every home around the world, in every library, in every classroom, and on the bookshelves of every major academic center and university in the world, as well as in the personal offices of every professional in the world who deals with people, be they doctors, nurses, psychologists, counselors, educators, lawyers, public relations firms, human resource personnel, media personnel (including TV and movie producers, journalists and reporters), and in the hands of just about everyone else interested in improving the quality of their life experience.

As a physician who treats not only physical maladies but also people with mental and emotional problems, I can't imagine a more effective or powerful prescription for health than the daily reading of even one or two pages of this beautiful book!

Arthur H. Brownstein, M.D., M.P.H.
Assistant Clinical Professor of Medicine
John A. Burns School of Medicine
University of Hawaii at Manoa
Author, *Healing Back Pain Naturally* (Harbor Press, 1999); *Extraordinary Healing* (Harbor Press, 2005)

☼

Elan Sun Star's newest book entitled *Smile* is brightly colored, beautifully displayed and filled with a brilliant blending of enlightening, uplifting and deeply meaningful images and messages captured from his inspired heart.

It is assured to add "face value" to anyone's life and smile.

Dr. John F. Demartini
www.demartini.com
Corporate lecturer/seminar leader
Featured in the international hit film, *The Secret*
Author of *The Breakthrough Experience—A Revolutionary New Approach*; *Amazing Life in 60 Days*; *Count your Blessings*; *Lessons for Life*; *Secrets of Immortality*; *Inspiration*; *Wisdom of The Oracle*; *Sacred Journey*; *From Stress to Success*

☼

Genuine smiles reflect perhaps the most crucial renewable human resource of our times—positive emotions.

As they accumulate and compound, genuine smiles and heartfelt positive emotions transform people and communities for the better.

In this unique book/website, *Smile!*, Elan Sun Star, the author, weaves strands of science and culture together with his photographic art to create an inspiring human tapestry. You can hardly prevent yourself from being moved and transformed by these images of profound beauty, joy and hope. Savor and enjoy!

Barbara L. Fredrickson, Ph.D.
Professor of Psychology, University of Michigan,
Ann Arbor, Michigan
Winner of the *Sir John Templeton
$100,000 Positive Psychology Award*

☼

I travel around the world, and from many people that I encounter, one of the most frequent questions that is asked is: "If you were to choose a place to live or to visit next, where would you like for it to be?"

Each time, I feel that it is not the place that makes it wonderful, but the smiling people that I meet in these places that I visit.

The good energy and smiles that I receive from people when I visit places is what I remember the most. When I think about all the people that I have met, I wonder how many *smiles* I have encountered.

No matter how beautiful the land is, if there are no *smiles*—I do not want to go, and vice versa.

Smile and good HADO...this is what makes my work worthwhile, and I feel that I am contributing towards a more peaceful world."

Dr. Masaru Emoto
Author of *The Hidden Messages in Water*
Featured in the hit film
What the Bleep Do We Know?

☼

The soulful art of Elan Sun Star is very transformational.

His images open the mind and expand the heart.

Arielle Ford, *www.fordsisters.com*
Author and publishing industry publicist expert
(Clients include Deepak Chopra; Wayne Dyer;
Jack Canfield and Mark Victor Hansen;
Neale Donald Walsch; Marianne Williamson;
Dr. Dean Ornish, M.D.; Louise Hay, and more.)

☼

The first act of diplomacy and world peace should be a *Smile*...you should give and receive as many *Smiles* as you can.

I've learned that a *Smile* is the universal language uniting all people.

One of the greatest gifts you can give as well as receive is a *Smile*. And to think it costs you nothing.

Sometimes when our world is upside down, our smile is upside down. Time for a somersault or handstand or just read *Smile!*

Only bodybuilders should frown—since experts tell us it takes more effort and muscles to frown, they are just muscle-building. Everyone else will find it easier to *Smile*.

Congratulations again on a fantastic book. Just think—if my ancestors had started my name with S instead of ending it with s, my name would be Smile instead of Miles!

Robert Miles
Author of *Warren Buffett Wealth*

☼

If you wake up with a smile or a frown, then your day will be accordingly.

Obviously so much of life is how we perceive it, and if you perceive it with a smile, then you will probably be a lot happier. Read this book *Smile!* and see why!

Fred Hemmings
Senator, Hawaii State Legislature
Worldwide surfing legend and pioneer

☼

Simple. Clear. Refreshing. Illuminating. Uplifting. Stimulating. Sincere. Relevant. Practical. True. Open this book—*Smile!*—and let it touch you. It will make your day.

Alan Cohen, *www.alancohen.com*
Author of *A Deep Breath of Life*; *Relax Into Wealth*;
The Dragon Doesn't Live Here Any More; *I Had It All the
Time*; *Dare To Be Yourself*

☼

It is good to note that smiling has good physiological effects.

Anson Chong, Senator from Hawaii

☼

…Smile?

I always tell people who come to pray in my synagogue that it doesn't matter if they know the words or melodies, as long as they keep a smile on their face as they seek to access the Divine.

The joyous spiritual energy of the universe is *God's Smile*—and as long as we smile, we open the gates of heaven and connect to God's love.

Read this book *Smile!* and keep smiling!

Rabbi Michael Lerner, Editor, *Tikkun Magazine*
www.tikkun.org/rabbi_lerner
Chair, The Network of Spiritual Progressives,
www.spiritualprogressives.org

☼

In this beautiful book, *Smile!*, Elan Sun Star shows the world how to refine its greatest asset: the human smile.

This work is thorough on the subject of smiling and instructs as well as inspires. This simple skill (smiling) can change your life as well as the lives of others who come into your visual range.

Read this book and smile at someone today.

Tim Sanders, www.timsanders.com
Author of *The Likeability Factor: How to Boost
Your L-Factor and Achieve Your Life's Dreams*
and *Love Is the Killer App.*
New York Times and international bestseller

☼

In my lifetime of traveling the world I have been every-where and seen everything, and I can tell you that I know that the human smile and what it brings is priceless for us all! Since I have traveled around the world 13 times, spoken and been on radio and television thousands of times in the past 55 years, I know a lot about human psychology, and I can tell you that there is nothing as healthy as a smile to refresh the spirit and the heart of anyone you meet.

And if you meet someone without a smile, please give them one of your own… they will most often pass it on.

My dad, Paul C. Bragg, who was known for his smile, was the father of the health movement and originator of health food stores.

He inspired millions to live a healthy lifestyle with the Bragg Crusades and Bragg Health Books worldwide. Everyday he woke up with a smile and went to bed with a smile. He loved life, and he had *agape* love for everyone!

This wonderful book *Smile!* is very well researched and packed full of healthy tips and stories and the most astounding information on why the smiles we give and receive daily are so powerful!

Your smile is powerful because it is instantly effective to bring a healthy welcome to all receiving your smiles.

Wherever I go, throughout the world, smiles are so important. Whether I'm at the Beach Boys' homes, Clint Eastwood's, Steve Jobs', or the United States White House, I feel my smile gives a welcome from my spirit and mind and heart to all I greet!

Successful people have one thing in common: they all know and respect the power of their smiles and the smiles in their lives.

We all know from a lifetime of personal experience that a smile is our greatest and best asset!

This book *Smile!* is destined to change the world for the better. Read *Smile!* and let it change your life!

Patricia Bragg, N.D., Ph.D.
Health and lifestyle educator to world leaders,
Hollywood stars, American business giants,
U.S. Presidents and champion athletes

☼

The book *Smile!* is simple, powerful, effective and scientifically based. Look in your mirror and try it!

I have been practicing cosmetic dentistry for over 15 years now, and I can say without any hesitation that the smiles that result from my corrective surgery and dental enhancements transform the lives of my clients.

The resulting beautiful smile I produce in my patients with corrective procedures brings happiness and a belief in themselves that they never had before.

Ohiro Yawamoto
Cosmetic dentist and oral surgeon

☼

The book *Smile!* has all the reasons I love to renew a person's smile in my dental practice. One can't help but smile and feel warm and fuzzy while seeing the pictures and reading the text.

Elan Star has found a unique way of capturing those experiencing this creation—smile.

A smiling face causes all to smile that see it and feel good.

My clients are always overjoyed to see their new smile and they know that the rest of their lives they will have a fantastic greeting in their smile wherever they go.

A smile from the heart is contagious, and your *Smile!* book spread to my heart and made me smile.

Dr. Paul Tanaka, DDS
Honolulu, Hawaii

☼

As the conductor for the Moscow Chamber Orchestra and traveling around the world guest-conducting, I see that the human smile is enlivening, transforming and inspiring, just as the music I conduct and perform.

In Russia and around the world, music and smiling are universal languages common to all cultures and people and to young and old alike. Music is the "language of the soul," and this book *Smile!* is a fine composition with the same ability to transform your spirit and your life.

Smile! is a symphony/concerto of inspiring information and research that will make your heart sing. Just as the famed Stradivarius violins were crafted by a Master for exceptional, unparalleled abilities, so too an authentic smile can transform and entrance the world around you. Read *Smile!* to find out why.

Constantine Orbelian
Conductor and director,
Moscow Chamber Orchestra

☼

It's been said that everyone smiles in the same language. And it's true. Smiling not only makes us and others feel good, it also bridges across the divides that can make us feel isolated.

Smiling is not only a step toward health and happiness, but a step toward world peace. This is a wonderful book.

John Robbins
Author of *Healthy at 100,*
Diet For A New America,
and *The Food Revolution*

☼

Imagine, a whole book all about smiling. You won't find another like it anywhere.

The author of this book—Elan Sun Star—is a Smilemaster, a generator of smiles.

The smiles in this book will set off an infinite cascade of smiles that can arrive anywhere, anytime.

Dr. David Chamberlain, Ph.D.
Association for Prenatal & Perinatal Psychology
Author of *The Mind of Your Newborn Baby*

☼

A book of smiles is a gift to everyone, for as someone said, "Everyone smiles in the same language."

From research we have conducted at the Institute of HeartMath, we know that a genuine smile, while shown on the face, emanates from the heart and is an expression of our complete inner and outer selves.

This collection *Smile!* should gladden everyone's heart—and thus lead to more smiles!

Rollin McCraty, Director of Research
The Institute of HeartMath—*www.heartmath.org*

☼

What the Dalai Lama, Shirley Temple, Nelson Mandela and Joan Lunden already know, a smile is our inherent gift of happiness. This book *Smile!* is a wonderful reminder of what is so easily forgotten, yet so essential to life.

Luke Seaward, Ph.D.
Author of *Stand Like Mountain, Flow Like Water*
and *Stressed Is Desserts Spelled Backward*

☼

...For decades Elan Sun Star's brilliant photography created a sense of joy and well-being for those lucky enough to see his work. Now Sun has taken his art to a new level!

Elan's new book *Smile!* combines the healing message of smiling to prove the power of the human smile with the beauty of the world through his camera lens and insights.

Smile! is literally a *magical blend* of insightful interviews with researchers, poets, physicians and philosophers..."

Mo Siegel, Founder of *Celestial Seasonings*
Board of *Whole Foods*

☼

A smile can allow us to activate our higher reasoning centers for our own well-being.

A smile does just that—it assures those who see the smile to know that it is possible to respond to a tense proceeding with an open and resourceful attitude. Read *Smile!* and transform your stress. It works for me in the courtroom.

Steve Slavit, Prosecutor
L.A. County District Attorney

☼

Much of our time is spent working so diligently at improving ourselves and our lot in life.

I am among those in the thick of it, coaching others to do so as they discover their ho'ohana, their on-purpose intention and passion in the work they do, as a celebration of the *aloha* spirit naturally innate in them.

I often find that we make it so much harder than it has to be; however, now we have *Smile!* and inspiration for more aloha with ease.

Sun has given all of us a magnificent gift with his book, for he has helped us understand that smiling is a way to share our aloha instantly and so naturally; he has given us more than enough proof that we *must* smile more for our own well-being in doing so, and he shows us through pictures which speak volumes in their contagiousness of spirit, inspiring us so joyously.

Smile! and know the joy you were meant to feel in each living moment.

Rosa Say, Founder and
head coach, *Say Leadership Coaching*
Author of *Managing with Aloha, Bringing Hawaii's Universal Values to the Art of Business*

☼

From Picasso's *Guernica* on, the visual arts of the 20th Century appeared mostly dedicated to portraying the deepest horrors of human experience around the planet. Offsetting that almost single-handedly, here in the early 21st, is photographer-essayist Elan Sun Star, whose works of transcendent beauty and energy are a ceaseless inspiration to mind, body and spirit.

A prime example of this is his latest colorful and informative book, *Smile!*, which I challenge you to peruse without generating many smiles of your own.

I hope he is a trend...Smiles are.

Win Wenger, Ph.D. — *www.winwenger.com*
Author of national bestseller, *The Einstein Factor*

☼

At last, a book to make us smile! This lovely book by Elan Sun Star demonstrates through both research and photographs the power of a genuine smile to uplift our spirits and help heal us. Whether it is directed toward others or ourselves or is simply an expression of our innermost being, a genuine smile says 'yes' to the miracle and mystery of love and life.

Dennis Lewis, *www.dennislewis.org*
Author of *The Tao of Natural Breathing*

☼

Elan Sun Star is an advocate of living life from love and fun while deeply caring for others.

Because of his deep interest and extensive knowledge in alternative health and healing modalities, many people seek his advice and guidance.

Elan Sun Star's new book, *Smile!,* which explores the tremendous benefits of smiling, is a must read for anyone interested in their own health.

When I teach stress management programs to corporations and their executives, I tell participants to look in the mirror and have a good smile and allow that to grow into a laugh.

This automatically sends a speedy message to the brain that everything is ok, which produces endorphins and other positive hormones while offsetting the negative effects of daily stress.

Smiling is not created by some occurrence or as the result of great and joyous conditions. Great and joyous conditions are created as the results of smiling. Belief precedes and produces experience.

Smiling is a state of mind which will make you happy. Don't wait to smile and don't wait to get a copy of *Smile!*

Jeff Gero, Ph.D.
Program Director for the *Center for Wellbeing*
Creator of *The Success Over Stress Program*
Author of *Secrets to Success at Work*

☼

Heart disease is largely preventable with daily activity, a healthy diet and a positive outlook on life and actions like **smiling.** Although the latter is all too often underemphasized, recent studies suggest that positive emotions may indeed benefit the heart, and smiling increases positive emotions in many ways.

Thus, while we continue to explore the intricate relationship between the mind and cardiovascular system, Elan

Sun Star's *Smile!* puts forth an outstanding and powerful testimonial for optimism, hope and connecting with others.

Needless to say, reading this book and **smiling** will do wonders for your heart and overall sense of well-being.

Michael Miller, MD, Director,
Center for Preventive Cardiology
University of Maryland Hospital, Baltimore, Maryland

☼

The greatest gifts are those that uplift the heart, nourish love, heal the spirit and inspire joy. Elan Sun Star brings us such a gift with his new book/web site: the book of *Smile!*

Sun's stunning photographs, filled with lush colors and sun-brightened faces, are complemented by a text that sheds light on the nature of something very near and dear to us all: the smile. In this book, we are reminded of the many healing benefits of a genuine smile. We learn about the effects of a smile on our physiology, read the words of scientists and poets, and are drawn toward the vision of a smiling, peaceful world.

This book is more than a fun read... it's an uplifting experience. If you got out of bed on the wrong side this morning, this is a book for you! The many smiles beaming at you from the pages of Sun's book will inspire you to respond in kind. Even those who don't read English will be uplifted by Sun's artful photography. I speak from experience. As I explored the book of *Smile!* together with my Chinese husband, a *qigong* master from Shanghai, he affirmed with a grin, "Smile, be happy -- this is TONIC NUMBER ONE!"

We found ourselves smiling broadly at the book of *Smile!* and agreed that all who peruse it with a willing heart will become positively infected with uplifted spirit and a fresh infusion of joy!

Katherine Orr and **Master Qing Chuan Wang**
www.wudangqigong.com

☼

In my work as a practicing medical intuitive, I work in co-ordination with doctors and other healers by first bringing to awareness the possible underlying causes of disease and pain.

Smiling is indeed a personal choice to look at life and the healing process in a positive and therefore constructive manner, which is tremendously supportive to the process of transforming of disease into ease and thus to health.

In this new book *Smile!* there is a wealth of fantastic facts on the power of smiling to transform our physical, mental and emotional health as well as our relations. Read *Smile!* and smile!

Cay Randall May, Medical Intuitive
Author of *Pray Together Now*

☼

Elan Sun Star has gathered the latest research and interviews on smiling and tethered it to his amazing inspiring images of smiling beings, creating a radiant book of inspiration and hope.

Energetically an authentic smile brightens the aura or subtle energy body and promotes heart-to-heart connection.

In my work with Barbara Brennan's techniques and direct perception of the human radiant aura, I can see and palpate this energy.

It is bright and colorful in healthy people with good attitudes and low and dull in people with distorted health and perceptions.

Sun Star's book illustrates what 'good medicine' exists in a smile.

In this world currently so impacted with negativity, war, hunger, disease, disaster, may we commit to the daily practice of smiling as a universal measure of love, peace, and joy.

A smile is a harmless yet very powerful and healing measure, which energetically and spiritually raises the planetary vibrational levels and promotes world peace.

This book *Smile!* can speak to you on many levels.

Dr. Ruey Jane Ryburn
Healer and professor emeritus,
University of Hawaii School of Nursing
Graduate founder, *Sacred Path Healing*, Honolulu

☼

A smile carries many messages in its upturned mouth. It warms us with its "yes." Smiling instills us with its message of acceptance.

Smiling inspires us with its amusement, giving us a magic passport into the world of Thalia, the Muse and guiding spirit of inspiration, creativity and comedy.

She wears a smiling mask and invites us to join her. What better place to visit? Read this book *Smile!* and you will know why and how.

Hob Osterlund, RN, MS
Health, Humor and Hospitals,
Queen's Hospital, Honolulu, Hawaii
Producer, *www.chucklechannel.com*

☼

WOW!! An entire book about smiles. How great is this classic penned by Elan Sun Star! I'm still smiling.

After I had broadcast NBA basketball for some 35 years, Elan Sun Star's *Smile!* brought many things to mind that certainly tied it in to the world of competitive sports. As I turned the pages, it brought to mind the many unforgettable smiles of some of pro basketball's greatest players:

Sports Hall of Famer **Connie Hawkins** possessed a great "child-like" smile. **Dr. J. Julius Erving** had plenty to smile about. And how about the sensational smiles of such super stars as **Michael Jordan** and **Magic Johnson**. The thing I noticed with all of them is their smile.

Thru the years I can't tell you how many of pro basketball's great coaches used "smiles" to encourage their players. During time-outs after the x's and o's have been discussed, so many coaches send their players back on the floor with a smile and the phrase, "OK, let's go...and let's have some fun!"

Let me borrow a couple of lines from Sun Star:

A smile says: "We're on the same team."

A smile says: "Let's create win-win and let's do this together." Remember...WINNERS, SMILE!!!!!!

That's why they win.

Al McCoy
Sports Broadcaster for the NBA, Phoenix, Arizona

☼

A book on smiling is a necessity in a world of hostility, selfishness and alienation. Elan Sun Star is opening the gates to the simplicity of joy, to how a smile can change a face, a state of mind, a life. We have a choice to sink into the fathoms of negativity or simply open our hearts and let love lead the way.

Sun Star's photography is a necessary counter-balancing force to the dark messages we daily receive from newspapers and television and media. Sun Star is dedicated to capturing with his camera the light of life and interviews with leading experts of our day on this neglected and primary subject, Smiling.

Xanya Sofra-Weiss, Ph.D.
Neurophysiologist and Clinical Psychologist, Author

☼

"Dare to Be Different—Smile."

By Peter Ragnar

There was only one person in the grocery aisle that day. I slowly progressed toward her with my cart, and our eyes met. As if I were meeting an old dear friend, I smiled broadly. She returned the gesture. We stood speechless in a timeless moment; then, unexplainably, but most naturally for old acquaintances, we hugged. When we released each other, her face pinked, as if she was embarrassed by her actions, and she quizzically asked, "Do I know you?" I replied, "I don't think so."

We went our separate ways as if nothing had happened, but you would be wrong to conclude that. It happened in a flash, but when you touch another's heart, it lasts forever. I remember the first few lines of a poem by Dennis Waitley: "Is there anything more to life than this, a baby's smile, a loved one's kiss…"

Whenever I see a bright-eyed baby smile, I see the joyous innocence that brightens even the sun's rays. When I see poor souls who have lost their smiles, it compels me to give them one of mine. Would you do the same? A smile isn't worth much until you give it away. Seeds planted in the hearts of strangers who are long out of sight become flowers passed on to another.

Once upon a time, there was an isolated village inhabited by two warlike clans. They had fought bitterly for longer than any of the living could remember. They argued over secular beliefs; they argued over religious doctrines; they argued over histories none could remember. They had become a sad and serious people who were joined together by only one thing: in that arid landscape, there was little water except the one well they shared in common.

One day, a traveling stranger happened upon the village. He was suddenly confronted by the tribal elders, who demanded a reason for his visit. Smiling broadly, he replied, "I'm a sower of seeds that become happiness trees."

"Happiness trees, you say?" objected one of the elders. "Look at this sandy soil. Can't you see how dry it is? What would you expect to grow in this? Are you mad to come here? What kind of seeds do you have that can grow without water?"

The stranger pulled a small pouch from his pack and answered, "Certainly not without water will they grow." Saying that, he threw the seeds into the village well.

"How dare you!" shouted one elder. "Perhaps he has poisoned our water!" shouted another. "We must taste the water to make certain." They all agreed. "But who will drink first?" "Make the stranger drink first!" shouted someone else.

"Here, let me show you," said the stranger as he lowered the bucket into the stone well. He lifted it back up and scooped water into his open palms, then drank, smiled broadly, and began to chuckle. Quickly, one after

Introduction

another, the villagers began testing the water. Then a strange thing happened.

The village chief began to smile for the first time anyone could remember. His smile broadened as he looked at his lifelong tribal adversary, who couldn't help returning the smile. By now, it was contagious: everyone was smiling. They asked the stranger what the seeds were made of. The stranger explained, "The seeds are made of forgetfulness. When we forget about all the things that divide us, the whole world will smile!"

It is said that nobody needs a smile as much as those who have none left to give. If you've ever visited a foreign land where you didn't know the language, you know that everyone knows the language of a smile. There is a certain electricity that is instantly felt when you smile.

Do you want to test that? The next time you're introduced to someone new, smile broadly and put your heart into your smile. Then, say silently to yourself, "I really like you." When you do that, you'll discover you're not only smiling with your lips, but also with your eyes; they will emit magical sparkles of light. Those sparkles are the seeds that grow happiness trees, because in moments like these, differences are all forgotten.

Remember, it takes just one little smile to make someone's day. It's like life handing you a bouquet, and then all day long you give flowers to others. In fact, this is a really heartwarming thing to do. Go to your florist and get a huge bouquet, and give every one of those flowers away. Say to everyone you give a flower to, "I'm so in love with life today, I want to give this flower away." They may think you odd, but that's okay—dare to be different and smile.

I say dare to be different, because the world can be filled with sadness for many people. If you feel blue and make the decision to wear a happy smile, the change can be magical. As studies will suggest, it's almost impossible to stay in a down mood when the corners of your mouth turn up.

I don't think there are any of us who have not felt the discouragement of broken dreams, lost love, illness, and those tragedies and challenges so common to our lives. Have you ever been in a public meeting or business gathering where the tone was serious and somber, and then you spied that special someone who lit up the room with their smile? Could that special someone be you? Despite the gravity of the situations we may face, wearing an up or down expression is always a choice. Happy faces heal. So, will you dare to be different?

The lyrics of the old Turner and Parsons song "Smile" come to mind. In a moment you may just find yourself humming them. "Light up your heart with gladness, hide every trace of sadness; although a tear may be ever so near, that's the time you must keep on trying. Smile, what's the use of crying? You'll find that life is still worthwhile, if you'll just—smile." Yes, it's so true that the world always looks brighter from behind a smile.

In fact, I'm smiling this very moment, at the fact that you'll be smiling too—that is, if I've done my job as the publisher of this uplifting book. Have you ever noticed that when people watch the world news on television, there's usually nothing to smile about? And think of this: The news is just about always made up of the same bad events happening to someone else. Now, what if you and I could get them to smile? Do you think those happy vibrations might just make someone's life a little better?

Introduction

An unknown poet wrote, "Smiling is infectious, you can catch it like the flu. Someone smiled at me today, and I started smiling too." So, when Elan Sun Star asked us if we would consider publishing <u>Smile</u>, what he was really asking was if we could get the whole world smiling too. If you believe that the power of a smile can be transforming and that this book has merit, would you do us and the rest of our human family a small favor? You already know what I'm asking, don't you? You can't hide that smile—yep! Get everyone a copy of <u>Smile</u>.

Someone wrote this about a smile: "None are so rich that they can get along without it, and none so poor that they cannot be richer for its benefits." So, again I say, dare to be different and smile! Smile and you'll enrich the lives of others. To enrich another's life is to enrich your own. Bringing joy to another's heart is the best way to bring peace to the world. What if you said to everyone you met, "I know something very good about you!" and then gave them a big broad smile?

In the words of Ella Wilcox, "You never can tell when you do an act just what the result will be, but with every deed you are sowing a seed, though the harvest you may not see. Each kindly act is an acorn dropped in God's productive soil; you may not know, but the tree shall grow with shelter for those who toil..."

Every time you smile, you're indeed planting a seed in the soil of the human heart. Please help us to gather a harvest of human hearts and smiling faces. Together we can make the world a lot brighter, if we but dare to be different and smile.

About the Author

Elan Sun Star is one of the world's most widely published global professional photographers, with thousands of brilliant and familiar covers and ad layouts in the world's top international publications and commercials.

His work is the top choice of many agencies in London, Tokyo, Honolulu, New York, Munich, Paris, Rio de Janeiro, Montreal, Los Angeles, San Francisco, Houston, Dallas, and other cities world-wide.

He is a well-known fine artist, classical keyboard performer, and pioneer in mind-body-spirit self-improvement modalities and alternative health.

He has traveled the world for 35 years, documenting optimum states of physiology and psychology while photographing incomparable people and action, interviewing and studying with many of the top pioneers in health and wellness and personal growth.

Sun has worked with such eminent people as Ann Wigmore of Hippocrates Health Institute, Dr. Bernard Jensen, and many others, as well as top motivational and peak-performance coaches and authors. From these rich experiences, Sun has synthesized a philosophy and teaching of simple and yet profound integration, which is reflected in his photography, his writings, and his speaking appearances.

Sun's writings reveal his comprehensive perspective, his deep caring and Renaissance style of contemporary wisdom, with profound messages of wellness, health, hope, and a world of unfolding possibilities.

His optimistic and yet informative text, garnered from extensive research, presents simple solutions for complex issues.

He has lectured extensively, and has been the subject of hundreds of radio and television shows in Europe, Japan, and the United States, with interviews in many magazines across the globe.

The hallmark of Elan Sun Star's appeal to millions through his photography and articles is his revelation of radiant hope portrayed in his photographic images and art.

Table of Contents

Foreword

Dr. David Allen, MD
The Longevity Clinic
Hollywood, California

Occasionally a book comes along that expresses something beautiful in a simple, refreshing, and delightful way. So it is with this book, *Smile!* Elan Sun Star's masterful photographs and informative text uplift the soul and make us all aware of how truly wonderful life is.

We learn how a simple facial movement—the contraction of just a few muscles in the face—can dramatically change our internal state.

What I mean by "internal state" is how we feel and think, what body sensations we have, our attitudes, and our points of view. We normally try to change this state in many different ways. These include psychotherapy, drugs, religion, sports, travel, and sex, just to name a few. Smiling costs less, you can do it all by yourself, and the results are immediate.

It is well known in medicine that people's attitudes toward their illnesses contribute to or take away from their recovery.

This became very clear to me during my internship at the Veterans' Hospital in Los Angeles. I examined a man who had come to the hospital complaining of jaundice, a yellowing of the whites of the eyes. He was found to have pancreatic cancer, and one week later when he missed his next appointment, I heard that he had died. This otherwise healthy-looking man died within one week of his diagnosis. This was shocking to me because I had seen many people with pancreatic cancer survive much longer. I will always remember the deep frown and slumped posture of this unfortunate man.

This was in stark contrast to a lecture during my second year of medical school at UCLA. The lecturer mentioned that for the last 10 years, he'd had colon cancer that had metastasized to his liver. He joked with a big smile on his face that he had an agreement with the cancer: "I don't bother it and it doesn't bother me."

The truth is, we have considerable control over our health. The field of psychoneuroendocrinology shows us how the brain and the body are connected through the endocrine or hormonal system.

Every thought and emotion that we have has a corresponding hormonal tone in our bodies. This tone can be health-enhancing or detracting. Sit up straight, let your eyes gaze upward slightly, smile, and see if you can feel bad. The simple act of smiling creates an emotional and hormonal tone that is life-generating and health-promoting.

I love to go to airports and see people being greeted by their friends and family. People who may rarely touch each other in other situations are smiling, hugging, and laughing. For a moment the cares of the day are forgotten, and love and connection dominate the moment. I can flip open this book to any page, view the pictures, and read the text, and for a moment the day seems to change. Life at that moment seems to slow down and become less complicated. I'm reminded of what's important in my life, and my priorities seem to come into a more healthy balance.

It is with great pleasure that I write the foreword for this inspiring book. As a medical doctor, I am dedicated to the mental and physical health of my patients. Elan Sun Star, a world-famous photographer and spiritual teacher, has made a contribution to the world and to the health of everyone. He reminds us how we can also contribute to the happiness of the world by simply smiling.

Smiling is contagious. One smile leads to another and another and another. Enjoy this wonderful book, give it to others, and create a wave of smiles that spreads to your family, friends, and communities and across the world.

☼

Foreword

Lee Pulos, Ph.D., ABPP

Every year, there are literally hundreds of books published on how to improve oneself, how to raise and strengthen self-esteem, or how to become more empowered by following the author's techniques and processes for change.

Implicit in this approach is the assumption that one is flawed or "less than." Also, these techniques and processes for change are usually "doing" or busy types of activities, not "being" states inherent in oneself. In the long run, they prove to be unsatisfactory because they miss the essence of the quality of living—how to enjoy the authentic, natural qualities of life already inside you.

Elan Sun Star has written and illustrated an enchanting and captivating book that falls under the aegis of an emerging new field on the subjective state of well-being, positive psychology, and the science of happiness.

He has brilliantly combined breathtaking photographs that invite the spirit to dazzle and dance with thoughtful and provocative commentary by leading scientists and philosophers of our time in the fields of medicine, psychology, and the mind-body-spirit relationship.

Since the beginning of time, a smile has conveyed the message "I am friendly; there is no threat, we can get along." This message has been reinforced in many ways, from Proverbs 17:22 in the Old Testament, "A merry heart doeth good like a medicine," to the 17th-century doctor referred to as the English Hippocrates, Sir Thomas Syndenham, who wrote, "The arrival of a good clown exercises a more beneficial influence on a village than twenty asses laden with drugs."

More recently, it has been established that it is not necessary to laugh out loud to improve one's health and spirits. The changes in facial muscles when we smile trigger cortical-evoked responses that reflect positive signals in the brain. It takes 17 muscles to smile and 43 to frown. A typical adult will smile 15 to 20 times a day, while children smile or laugh 150 to 200 times a day.

Does this mean, as a nameless philosopher once said, that we are sadly moving from the happy ignorance of childhood into the sobering reality of adulthood? I discovered as I read through Elan Sun Star's book that his stunning and dazzling photographs and text ignited a re-enchantment with a deeper wisdom that resides in all of us—but perhaps we have forgotten that we know it. This remembering of smiles and their joy helped bring back many early memories from when my senses were more alive, colors were more brilliant, and all 125 million receptors in my eyes were participating in this new choreography called life.

A smile, of course, is the precursor to laughter, but triggers a similar range of physiological changes in the mind/body. For example, beta endorphins are released; these are not only "feel-good molecules," but they also suppress pain. Stress hormones such as cortisol and epinephrine are reduced dramatically when one is smiling and laughing. The production of immune cells increases, and antibody levels in the blood and saliva are elevated to the benefit of the individual smiling.

While smiling or looking at the world through optimistic filters may not totally eliminate the stresses of life, it does help distance us from stressful situations and dilute the effects of negative emotions.

Health care professionals throughout the country have started dispensing humor to help patients cope with surgery, pain, cancer, and other life-threatening conditions.

Many contemporary hospitals have special areas with televisions showing comedy programs or old movies on funny subjects and comedians to get the patients to smile and lose their grave expressions and despair. Patients are being visited by physicians and counselors dressed as clowns, and they are distributing comic books, games, and toys to increase rapport and motivate patients to participate more actively in their treatment program based on humor and smiling.

When people smile or laugh, it gets their minds off their illnesses and helps reframe stressful events so they can serve as a means of change. While physical attractiveness is a highly prized asset in most cultures, it has a very low correlation with joy and the pleasures of life. The same can be said for intelligence, which has practically no influence or effect on how much a person smiles to reflect an inner sense of contentment and happiness.

In an article on infant joy, Robert Lewis quotes an Apache fable in which the Creator of All That Is bestowed every gift on humans that they needed to live—movement, all five senses, and the ability to think and create—but something very important was still missing. It was not until the Creator provided humans with laughter and joy that this Creator could say, "You are all fit to live." The addition of laughter and joy completed the circle of wholeness and provided an antidote to the darker side of human emotions.

Unfortunately, as children grow older, we tend to de-hypnotize them from their natural, spontaneous, playful and zestful ways of being in the world. The emphasis shifts to becoming more serious and grown-up, which means replacing the smiles and fun-loving behavior with the demeanor of adults so they can "act their age." How sad, since joy and playfulness have a much deeper impact than the occasional feel-good moods of adulthood.

There is indeed considerable research to suggest that smiling is an inoculation of energy that ignites an enduring sense of buoyancy and well-being and fuels the ongoing perception that life is fulfilling, pleasant, and meaningful.

In a longitudinal study conducted with nuns in the 1930s, short personal essays the nuns wrote about their childhoods, their lives, and the events that led them to the convent were examined 60 years later. The nuns whose biographical sketches reflected positive emotional content, happiness, love, and hope lived up to 10 years longer and had significantly fewer diagnoses of dementia.

As John Milton wrote, "The mind...can make a heaven of hell, a hell of heaven." There has been a recent surge of interest in the strange, quirky world of quantum physics.

Physicists and metaphysicists are beginning to sound as if they are reading off the same page. That is, our visible reality is but a thin crust that percolates up from the vibratory realm, the frequency domain of the quantum world—*i.e.,* our basic reality. Every cell, molecule, and panorama of particles of the sub-atomic world is vibrating at different, mind-dazzling frequencies, dancing to its own inherent song or rhythm.

The law of attraction states that whatever you choose to give your attention or focus to causes you to emit a vibration or resonance and thereby attract a similar vibratory experience back into your life.

For example, there is a major vibrational difference between expressing appreciation (consonance) and expressing resentment or anger (dissonance), which can influence every cell and organ in your body, especially heart rate variability. Thus, one cannot create or attract love, health, or prosperity while subconsciously sending out conflicting vibratory messages of undeservability or unworthiness.

One of my clients described having major social anxiety and low self-esteem; he could not look anyone in the eye, as he felt he would be judged and people would see the "real worthless me," to use his words.

As part of the counterphobic strategy to deal with this issue, he decided to act as if he had overcome his social phobia. With great trepidation and fear, he chose to look a complete stranger in the eyes and smile while walking down the street. To his astonishment, the person smiled back. Still experiencing some dread and anxiety, he repeated that simple social signal on successive days, and almost always was rewarded with a favorable look, grin, or smile.

At our last session, he looked me in the eyes and greeted me with a smile and a firm handshake. How could a simple change of facial expression turn adversity into triumph? Is there an inherent human capacity that can burst forth and dilute or metabolize away the most difficult and challenging circumstances? An effortless smile?

In the past 30 years, 90,000 scientific papers were published on depression, anger, and anxiety, but just over 4,000 papers were published on joy and happiness. Over 2,000 years ago, Aristotle was convinced that, more than anything else, men and women seek happiness and joy. Fortunately, Elan Sun Star has captured the wondrous essence of the philosopher's wisdom and has chosen to illustrate and breathe life into this vital element of the human condition.

Smile! is a visual feast that radiates joy and brilliant optimistic images that will continue to resonate in and illuminate your heart and spirit long after you have read it.

About the author: Lee Pulos, Ph.D., ABPP, is a clinical psychologist, lecturer, and the author of *The Biology of Empowerment* and *The Power of Visualization.* See his website, www.drpulos.com.

☼

Part 1

Smile for All Sorts of Reasons

Simplify

Smiling…effective, simple, and powerful

by Elan Sun Star

"…The simpler the better…"

Why would anyone choose a complicated life when a simple, joyous version would be so much more fun?

In the fields of psychology and medicine, there are innumerable theories and practices aimed at self-improvement and at improving one's state of mind as well as social coping skills. Many of these practices have real merit, yet just as many are hopelessly complicated and time-consuming, and usually expensive to boot.

I have studied innumerable varieties of self-improvement psychology that help one attain optimum or peak performance and self-improvement, and I still find that the premise of Occam's Razor is the best measure: "The simpler the proposal or theory, the better!"

This principle works better for practical applications than the more complicated and esoteric therapies that are sometimes controversial and protracted and hard to practice for the average person.

Since a lifetime of emotional therapy or even intellectual study is just not possible for the majority of humans, there is an obvious need to complement and supplement conventional psychological practices with simple, to-the-point additions. The measure of any therapy or practice does not lie in how expensive it is, or how long it takes to achieve success.

Clearly, *more* is NOT *better*!

After years of reading research papers and books and listening to tapes by a variety of clinical specialists and self-improvement gurus, I have concluded that quite often a simpler method is much more effective and transformational for an individual.

Why is this true? The obvious element seems to be basic human nature. If something takes a lot of time or is beyond the intellectual grasp of the average person, there is only a slim chance that people will follow through on it. And if something is too expensive, there is even less chance of commitment. People just don't want to take the time. They have to choose where they make their commitments.

 Whether they are healthy or not, people may want to change and transform their mental, emotional, and physical states, but they are just not equipped with enough time or comprehension to stick with the standard clinical methods of bringing about change in a healthy personal and social attitude. There are just too many factors working against them, even if they are sincerely seeking change and healthy new growth and integration within themselves and in society.

What, then, is an alternative modality likely to be? Alternative and complementary medicine, including standard body-mind-spirit techniques, can be just as demanding and overwhelming to most people as the more traditional route of doctors and psychologists. It is difficult to make the fundamental changes that are necessary to experience the first steps in transformation and healing.

The first step is the foundation for transformation. The difficult first steps are essential, because they entail believing in oneself before going on to progressively more integral and expanded ways of becoming what we might call a "whole person."

If the average person experiences failure repeatedly, or sometimes even just one time, this can close the door to expectations of success and lead them to abandon the process of self-improvement. People give up when it is hard or if they fail. It is as simple as that! It is human nature.

What is the alternative?

Simplify!

Remind people that they already know how to make great changes—changes that are not only simple, but already known to bring results. Simple things that already make them feel good and make others around them feel good, day in and day out.

The answer lies in the integration of basic and simple responses to life and experience—responses that we have every day. The answer is characterized by a common global understanding, an innate positive response—an action that is usually without thought but can transform a person's mind, emotions, and yes, even biochemistry.

Psychologist Martin Seligman in his work with optimism, along with other notables in the field of "new psychology," has ushered in what is today known as "positive psychology." The key finding of positive psychology is that individuals who respond positively to the challenges of life and relationships and, yes, to their own inner mental and physical states, are much more likely to become healthy, functioning members of society. Their families are more functional, and they tend to be much happier than those who dwell on the negative aspects of life.

In this book, *Smile!*, I have interviewed some of the top names in contemporary psychology and medicine and related fields of research to offer a broad spectrum of insights into the activity we know simply as "smiling."

These researchers tell us that smiling is anything but simple. The smile results from complex biochemical, bioelectrical, and emotional-mental factors, although its practical nature may have evolved to be simple over the last several millennia. That is why it has proliferated globally as the "universal language."

Smiling says so much, with so few words. Prenatal research shows that the smile is present even before birth, and definitely at birth in good, healthy, pleasant births. Smiling is not something you have to study arduously and learn over a period of time: it is instinctual and primal. Plus, it says good things about the smiler to those who receive the benefits of the smile.

Immediate and intuitive responses to challenges in life, or responses that are easy to learn and easy to implement, are the ones that win over in the evolutionary scheme of things. Why? Life must be simple, or else it will appear to be too complex and overwhelming.

 Thus, things that make us feel comfortable and safe, loved and loving, become the criteria by which entire civilizations and whole species adapt over time. We live in a unique time in history wherein the factor of time seems critical, and though the frantic pace of life may be no more than a personal interpretation for a majority of the people, it does serve to complicate life, to obscure the basic goodness, the wholeness, and the inherent simplicity of the "good life."

Nearly everyone living today says in one way or another, "Life has to be simpler, easier. Life has to make me feel good."

Smiling fits the global demand for simple solutions.

When an individual relates to others in society, the smile is a simple innate response that works to bring about healthy cooperation. It is essential.

There is nothing so powerful and practical as a smile— nothing that can so easily bring about harmony and respect, nothing that so universally elicits a positive response from others, as the simple act of smiling.

Since smiling is an integral part of social life, and in some societies an integral part of spiritual and health practices, it is already a time-proven solution. A smile can transform an individual into an optimally self-actualized person.

A smile costs nothing. It takes no time, literally, and it is a universal currency known in every culture around the globe. The smile has the power to bring about a healthy personal attitude. The biochemistry and emotions behind a smile even serve to optimize social interactions!

* * * * *

Many researchers were interviewed for this book. They come from fields as diverse as medicine and psychology, mind-body-spirit interactions, business and negotiations, and entertainment. Together, they make the simple smile into a rich tapestry.

Many of those who were interviewed for *Smile!* have their own insights into the positive value of smiling, both for those who do the smiling and for those who receive the smile. The doctors, psychologists, and other professionals who were interviewed already employ smiling as an effective technique for bringing about healing and a sense of profound well-being in their clients, patients, business associates, and colleagues.

In *Smile!* it is revealed that heartfelt love can easily be expressed through the well-known activity of smiling. No big surprise there. But the interviewed experts will also tell you how the smile can be used to great benefit at home or at the office, and even in global peace negotiations. Smiling is beneficial. It is a time-tested method of obtaining positive results.

I urge you to read and reread this collection of interviews and personal insights into the comprehensive value of smiling—the cost-effective and globally accepted pan-acea for "all that ails thee." I welcome you to further investigate the extensive published literature in medi-cine, psychology, and the social sciences that leaves us without a doubt that "smiling is the best medicine."

Research disproves the old belief that one has to have a reason to smile first! We can create our own reason to smile by smiling first: a pre-emptive smile!

Our modern lives demand direct knowledge and intui-tive thinking. A healthy response to life and a healthy attitude are a must to maintain an optimum lifestyle and a healthy state of mind and body.

I am positively certain that you will find *Smile!* to be a wealth of unique information and inspiration on your path of self-discovery. In fact, the practice of smiling is the most powerful way you can positively affect your own life, as well as the lives of all with whom you come in direct contact and, *most important*, those with whom you are in indirect contact!

Indirect contact?

Yes, as we spread what many call "the smiling virus" around the world, we defuse global antagonisms and misinterpretations and create an optimum "win-win" situation wherein the smile-giver and the one receiving the blessing of the smile both experience a state of wellness and joy, opening the door to extended dialogue.

Smiling may well be the medicine of the future, but it is here now and has always been available. It is practiced by newborns as well as centenarians, and it is practiced in every country in the world. A smile means nothing less than "YES!"

Welcome to a world worth smiling about.

Welcome to *Smile!*

Come Out Smiling:
David Chamberlain, Ph.D.

by Elan Sun Star

"Smiling from birth is a magical beginning.
I have seen smiling babies throughout the
world where they are born in favorable
circumstances. Whether in Russia or California
or France or Sweden or Thailand, a smile is a
language a baby can understand. Smile like a
newborn child and your life can begin."
—David Chamberlain, Ph.D.

After birth, we can see for ourselves that babies sometimes smile, especially when face to face with a smiling mom or dad. When a baby returns your smile, it is a wonderful demonstration of what babies can see and feel. But, "psychologists have had their doubts about these smiles for the last hundred years." That is the perspective of an unusual psychologist, David B. Chamberlain, Ph.D., who concentrates on studies of baby behavior during the earliest phase of their development—from conception to birth.

During the 20th century, Chamberlain says, theories about babies smiling after birth depended heavily on *how much brain* the babies had and *when* certain parts of the brain were definitely connected. From that viewpoint, newborn babies were judged to have insufficient brainpower to feel pain, have emotions, remember anything, *or have authentic smiles*. The first smiles after birth, therefore, were merely "reflexive" and void of personal meaning. (This is what they also said about baby cries and baby pain.)

Eventually, researchers agreed that true "social" smiling in mutual face-to-face interactions, like those of babies and parents, could be expected around six weeks after birth.

"I was dubious about this claim," Chamberlain confesses, "because at just 10 days after birth, I had a warm, smiling dialogue with my first son that ended in a responsive smile accompanied by a breath-catching gasp and small explosive sound that revealed both rapt attention and an effort to respond verbally."

This theory about not smiling until six weeks after birth began to erode when scientists seriously measured the behavior of babies born prematurely. These babies are 10 to 12 weeks younger than full 40-week newborns.

What these scientific explorers discovered, says Chamberlain, was that the *first* smiles were seen while premature babies were *dreaming*. Because they were out of the womb, it was easy to observe the rapid eye movements (REMs) that mark dreaming in sleep.

They also found that premature babies were really big dreamers. The density of smiling for them was 34 smiles per 100 minutes of REM time, versus 8.8 smiles per 100 minutes of REM time for full-term newborns.

Looking at the larger picture, researchers found that the amount of time we spend in REM states (dreaming) falls progressively through our life span, from eight hours per day in newborns to less than one hour per day in old age.

Chamberlain emphasizes that researchers were able to see and measure the opposite ways "preemies" reacted to particular dreams in their breathing, body movements, and facial expressions. Body language was dramatic: 10 to 15 seconds of writhing of the torso, limbs, and digits, accompanied by frowns and grimaces apparently associated with "bad dreams." In sharp contrast were the calm, smooth movements accompanied by smiling, reflecting what we would call "sweet" dreams. This revealing evidence not only demonstrated dreaming and smiling at younger ages, but clearly established dreams as qualitatively different and very personal in their effect.

Exactly how early can dreaming start? Regular ultrasound instruments have established first REMs as early as 21 weeks from conception. More recently, new 3-D high-speed ultrasound technology has given us a new kind of evidence confirming early smiling: close-up pictures of baby faces showing smiles as early as 20 weeks. Is smiling innate? Yes. Smiling is an innate response to feeling good, just as crying is a response to feeling bad.

Important evidence about this, Chamberlain reminds us, came from a pair of notable obstetricians in France and Sweden who began to look more closely at the emotional expressions on the faces of newborns. French obstetrician Frederick Leboyer was the first to take seriously the unhappy looks on the faces of uncounted hundreds of babies born under his own care. According to Chamberlain, this interest was undoubtedly sparked by a profound experience in personal therapy when he recalled his own birth. After this, Leboyer began to believe that newborn expressions were authentic and reflected how they truly felt at their births. He set out to change the standard birth protocols of his day and reinvent them to honor the *baby's* feelings. (Don't you wonder why thousands of other doctors before him had never thought of this?)

Details of the new plan were revealed in his book, *Birth Without Violence* (1974), which set a new standard for gentle birthing with low lighting, a quiet, reverential atmosphere in the birth room, and—ready for use at the appropriate moment—a womb-temperature bath. With every adjustment, Leboyer watched for a change in baby bodies and faces, and they finally appeared. Babies began to look peaceful and smile.

Meanwhile, over in Sweden the noted obstetrician Dr. John Lind was struck by the photos from France showing the anguished faces of babies at delivery.

Having delivered thousands of babies himself at Karolinska Hospital in Stockholm (without seeing faces like this), Lind felt something was amiss. To prove a point, he started taking photos of newborns in his delivery room until he had accumulated 130 of them. After analysis, it was clear that baby faces in Sweden were different from those in France and other Western countries!

The photos showed, not anguish and pain, but "curiosity and often great expectations," according to Lind (1978). This research spoke volumes about the good conditions for birthing in Sweden (at that time and still today) compared to most other countries. Babies know the difference; the proof is on their faces.

In faraway Thailand, the obstetrician Dr. Chairat Panthuraamphorn at Bangkok's Hua Chiew Hospital probably holds the world record for smiling babies. Why? Because of a systematic program of prenatal stimulation and enrichment that he offers couples beginning about halfway through pregnancy.

Mothers are encouraged to take time each day to have a warm bath, sit in a rocking chair, relax, look at a beautiful picture, and listen to classical Thai music. The doctor recommends abdominal massage three times a week, along with breathing exercises, visualizations of birth, a multi-sensory program of speaking and singing to the child, playing a game with a bell, and other activities to enhance bonding.

And the result? Graduates from this program have the highest frequency of both spontaneous and social smiles in the first week of life that has been reported anywhere in the world.

In America, smiling newborns are almost never seen! Why not? What are we doing wrong? Doctors here do not discuss this as a problem, nor do they look for anything different. Instead, the typical chorus of screams and cries at birth is accepted as normal. Doctors even congratulate babies when they cry strongly. In fact, crying is the only way for a baby to receive a full Apgar score—the ubiquitous measure of baby well-being in American medicine. Obviously, there is no campaign to lower the number of babies born in anger and pain and no plan to reward parents who give birth to smiling babies. Chamberlain has suggested that things might change if birth practitioners were rewarded for babies who smile during delivery or penalized financially for babies born screaming in protest!

But can we realistically expect babies to be born smiling? The answer to that question comes from the babies who do. These babies are teaching us something we have a hard time understanding—the fact that they *like* the way they are being treated at birth. Their smiles are not silly little reflexes, any more than their piercing cries are irrelevant to what we are doing to them.

All through gestation, babies practice perceiving the intimate world that surrounds them with the whole range of their senses. They know when dangerous things are happening to them and to their mothers and fathers, Dr. Chamberlain claims.

Babies also know when conditions are right. Consider the calm state of babies born in water. Photographs document how much better babies feel when their mothers have had the comfort of laboring in water, and when they have entered the world by passing from the amniotic "sea" to a larger pool and into their mother's waiting arms.

Chamberlain remembers a photo of a water baby on her mother's tummy, hand on the nipple and smiling ear-to-ear just seconds after birth. Water birth advocate and author Barbara Harper comments that these babies seem to know their mothers have had an ecstatic experience; they express total peace and wear a "thank you!" on their faces.

Chamberlain concludes: "In an age of violence, we do well to watch baby faces carefully and to believe what they are telling us.

In the past, we neither watched nor believed. We have not let baby faces determine the direction of obstetrical practice—in spite of the poetic and powerful warnings of Frederick Leboyer. We are still holding to the mistaken assumption that gruesome faces and angry screaming are 'normal.' This myth befits a violent society. But smiling babies have been trying to teach us a higher standard for birth: birth without violence as a foundation for life without violence.

Let's make smiling babies an urgent national priority. I believe it would make a huge difference in our personal happiness and in the health of our society."

☼

Humor Me

by Elan Sun Star

"Every time a man smiles, and much more when he laughs, it adds something to his fragment of life."

—*Laurence Sterne*

Laughing and humor are a magical part of smiling. No one would doubt that humor plays a hefty role in promoting "silly smile sessions." What is a silly smile session? It is a lot more than it sounds like.

In some of the biggest Fortune 500 companies in the world, silly smile sessions in the form of humor and laughter are utilized to stimulate team-building.

Volumes have been written on how to use humor. Books such as *Laugh and Learn* have shown how humor is the greatest tool to get people to smile, then to laugh, and ultimately, to start using both hemispheres of their brains. Connecting the left and right hemispheres through the corpus callosum makes us more effective creators.

The more uptight, anxious, worried, stressed, and workaholic we are, the more we cut ourselves off from the universe, and the more we dampen the synchronicities, magical connections, encounters, and seeming coincidences that change our lives, the more we retard the development of relationships and meetings that can change our lives and the lives of those we encounter for the better. If we're stressed and lacking a sense of humor, or if we have a frown, we tend to block that happy line of least resistance, that happy flow, that health-bringing smile.

Here's where smiling plays a giant role. You don't have to laugh uproariously and disconcertingly in a business meeting or at home, especially when people might mis-interpret the meaning—but you can give a gentle and authentic heartfelt smile. You can lift up the negotia-tions by giving a heartfelt smile. In other situations, when you're free to laugh, humor uplifts you.

Humor, smiling, laughter, intelligence, play, and health are all related because they support each other. They are interdependent. Laughter and humor are sometimes spurred by life's incongruities—circumstances that would confuse you if you tried too hard to analyze them.

How do comedians like Robin Williams and Jim Carrey get their audiences to laugh? They mix opposing ideas and themes in an unexpected way. They catch the audi-ence by doing something irrational or unexpected. That opens up the door. If their humor can make you laugh when you see it on the screen, it makes you wonder why you don't laugh when you see absurdities in your daily life.

 Successful humor leads to smiles and laughter. It's cathartic; it releases, it expands, it causes wheezes and coughs and gasping breaths, it reddens the face and increases the flow of blood to the skin. It blushes. You can't hold it back. It makes you fully alive. It is difficult, if not impossible, to tell a lie while you are genuinely laughing. Authentic smiling is the greatest truth serum there is. It leads to "authentic happiness," in the words of Professor Seligman.

Humor has a synonym—levity. Jocularity and humor equal levity. What is levity? Well, think of the word "levitation"—floating, flying, soaring, lifting, rising, levitating. Have you ever seen a magician on stage levitating his assistant?

There is an alchemy, a magical science behind the smile. It can infect the world with laughter, joy, and humor, which boost the functioning of the mind, the brain, and the intelligence (not all necessarily the same thing). When laughter and humor seem inappropriate, a smile is always appropriate; there's never a time when a smile is not appropriate.

You might ask, "What about a funeral, a death, or an accident?" You can always put forth a gentle, benevolent smile of acceptance and acknowledgment that something is working behind the scenes—a divine order, an acceptance of the soul that has passed on. A smile can communicate that an accident can be healed.

Think of Leonardo da Vinci's painting of the Mona Lisa. The unknown woman in the painting has an enigmatic smile that has intrigued artists, scientists, and laypeople for centuries. It is an expectant smile, one that is just beginning and is waiting for you to finish it. The Mona Lisa's smile invites you to add your own finishing touches to the corners of the mouth and the crinkles beside the eye.

Researchers over the last decade in Italy have developed a theory by using computers to study the few remaining self-portraits, sketches, and portraits of the artist Leonardo da Vinci.

The researchers have concluded that the structural basis for Mona Lisa's face was the artist himself, Leonardo! He is peering out through that face, playing a trick on you and inviting you to smile once you get the joke.

It wasn't really necessary for me to tell you that smiling is good for you. You already knew it. Your mother knew it when she smiled at you when you were born. Your father knew it when he smiled at you. And you smiled every time your intelligence learned something new, or when you learned how something worked.

Every time, you let out a little bit of a smile, even if it was only an inner smile. Maybe you didn't notice because you weren't looking in the mirror, and maybe nobody saw you or acknowledged it or told you, but every time you learned something new, there was a smile.

It's called the SMILE OF KNOWING.™

Universities have shown that humor increases test scores, including SAT scores, along with overall intelligence. So, even when you don't feel like smiling for someone else, smile for yourself, smile for me, smile for the world, smile for your brain, smile for your heart, smile for your health, smile for the future, and smile for everything, even if you don't feel it's perfect. Smile so that you can learn from it, because a smile is the best response to anything.

You don't have to know the science of electricity to turn on a light switch. You just need to flip the switch, and there is the light. You don't need to know all the research about smiling, intelligence, or humor, but it's nice to know that while some people are arguing the point, other people are laughing, playing, happy, and intelligent beings.

Remember, $E = mc^2$.

"E" stands for *energy* and enthusiasm. Enthusiasm comes from the Latin word *entheos*, meaning God (*theos*) saying, "This is energy, let's do it!" Enthusiasm, smiling, laughing, playing, humor—all of it leads to…

"M," which is *mass* in the mc^2 part of the formula. Mass is anything you want to create, anything you intend to do, and anything you love to do or want to do.

"C" is the speed of light. A smile moves faster than the blink of an eye! It warms the heart instantaneously!

Smiling is a powerful energy, not just a metaphor. That's why it happens all the time and catches you unaware. Thank God it's unpredictable. Thank God it happens even when you're trying to stop it.

☼

Is It Real?

by Elan Sun Star

"Whence that three-cornered smile of bliss?
Three angels gave me at once a kiss."
—George MacDonald

What do smiles really mean? You know the sign: you recognize true delight in a friend's face. It's no surprise that we're all put off by a false smile because it looks so fake. It's not the truth. Once we see the real thing, the fake becomes literally offensive and looks cold and harsh. Does this mean that certain smiles cover up the fact that there's not an authentic, heartfelt emotion of caring or real happiness behind the smile?

You cannot fake happiness, but you can create it within yourself, and when you do, you deeply touch everyone around you. Another Frenchman, 17th-century author and moralist Francois de la Rochefoucauld, had the idea, as he wrote:

> To win that wonder of the world,
> a smile from her bright eyes,
> I fought my King, and
> would have hurled
> the gods out of their skies.

If smiling doesn't feel right, just stand in front of the mirror and try out what looks like a smile. You don't have to be an actor to get into the mood. Just remember that even a forced smile will make you feel good by releasing endorphins and other feel-good biochemicals. The more you do it, the better you will get at it, whether you feel like smiling or not. One of the best times to smile is when you really don't feel like it, because doing it will make you feel better. Smiling will give you the natural painkillers to make it through any challenge you are facing, be it mental, emotional, or physical.

The smile is a learned response. The more you do it, the more it becomes natural. The more you do it, the better you feel and the more reasons you have to feel good and to smile.

So, you see, the reverse is true. Sometimes you have to smile when you don't feel like it, and maybe those corners of your eyes won't crinkle up, but you're still getting the effects you want, and it will be contagious, like laughter. Sooner or later, someone will smile at you, you'll smile back, and they'll smile back at you, and it will become a conditioned reflex. At that point, you have reached natural spontaneity and it is a real smile! Just keep at it!

What do you do when a photographer says, "Smile"? Some people say the word "cheese," which makes the corners of their mouth rise up. They say "cheese" to themselves and produce an artificial smile, a polite pose. Others are readily able to give a radiant, authentic smile.

Look at the photographs in a high school yearbook, as Martin Seligman has done, and you can easily identify these two types of smiles. One is genuine and one is make-believe. A genuine smile has been found to predict a person's level of happiness in later life. A genuine smile—a Duchenne smile—is the one element that allows us to positively respond to people in our environment and to signal to them that we welcome them into our space and our life.

Psychological researchers coded all of the photographs in a 1960s women's college yearbook and found that half of those smiling had a Duchenne smile. All of the students were subsequently interviewed at ages 26, 43, and 52 regarding the state of their marriages, their satisfaction with life, and their happiness levels. It was found that a higher percentage of the women with the genuine smiles—those showing real happiness in 1960—got married, stayed married, and reported a sense of personal well-being than the women who just gave polite half-hearted "fake" smiles. But remember, fake it till you make it.

When Professor Paul Ekman was measuring brainwave activity, he discovered that a spontaneous, authentic smile was accompanied by increased activity in an area of the brain known to be the seat of positive emotion. He also found that if a person intentionally produced an eye-crinkling smile, those same pleasure centers were activated, although not as intensely as with the spontaneous smile. Thus, the value of this "fake it till you make it" smile has been proven in the laboratory. Even if you are not doing the authentic, spontaneous, heartfelt Duchenne smile, you still get brain activity in the pleasure centers, producing positive emotions by just acting like you're smiling.

This is very significant research, because the more we smile, the better we feel; and thus, the more we attract people who want to be around us. When we feel happier and smile more, we attract more smiling people and make them feel good, so we all end up smiling and feeling better simply because each of us went ahead and tried to smile. Got all that?

Smiling is like bodybuilding: repetition works. So work those smiling muscles! It appears that we can make ourselves somewhat happier by smiling on purpose if we smile the right kind of smile.

Try to smile a Duchenne smile even if you're faking it. Look in the mirror when you have a fake smile, then smile with your eyes. You can see that it really looks like you're happy and you care, that you are truly displaying a good feeling—a good vibe—and this will bounce back to you.

Those who spread joy and happiness by smiling can't help but reap the rewards of joy, happiness, and smiles coming back from others.

☼

The Inner Smile

by Elan Sun Star

"Sometimes your joy is the source of your smile, but
sometimes your smile can be the source of your joy."
—*Thich Nhat Hanh*

The *inner smile* is a simple
yet profound meditation
based on Taoist and Chi-
nese meditation practices.
The inner smile can ease
emotional or physical tension and is quite natural
to all persons regardless of their philosophy in life. It is a
powerful relaxation technique that utilizes the expanding energy of happiness and joy and the good feelings
associated with smiling.

The inner smile communicates with the internal organs
of the body, with the "second brain" in the abdomen,
known as the *hara*, and with the universe as well.

The inner smile is centered on internally generating the
benevolent qualities of a genuine smile that we usually
offer to others through our faces and our body gestures.
The inner smile is an opportunity to offer a smile to
the whole being using an inwardly directed energetic
projection of the joy and healing qualities of an external
smile.

Let your body, your heart, and your other organs smile. As you redirect the energy of a smile inward, visualize the individual organs, yin/yang organ pairs, or your whole body smiling. This will generate endorphins, nitric oxide, growth hormones, DHEA, and other biochemicals that benefit the immune system and other systems within the body.

Here is how to generate an inner smile: Find a quiet place. Sit in a comfortable chair or in a seated meditation posture, or lie down on your back with your arms at your sides. Find whichever position you are most comfortable with. Many people integrate the inner smile into Hatha yoga practice.

Focus inwardly, closing your mind to outer distractions, and visualize a smile in your body, your lungs and large intestine, your heart and small intestine, your stomach and spleen, your kidneys and urinary bladder, your liver and gall bladder, your brain, your eyes, and your various other sense organs. Scan your body and relax any tension you may be holding. Let your spine rise from your pelvis as if a balloon were drawing you up. Draw your chin slightly in and keep your spine straight to allow the energy to flow.

Sense a feeling of natural happiness and joy, as though it emanates from behind your eyes or from another internal place such as your solar plexus. Some people like to visualize the inner smile generating initially in the heart, but use whatever feeling or visualization you have.

As you continue, visualize your inner smile cascading like a waterfall throughout your body, flowing down your spine into your heart and lungs, then your stomach and spleen, through your ribs, into your liver, kidneys, colon, intestines, and lower belly, down to your legs, and out through your feet.

The inner smile can be a complete meditation in itself, or a prayerful absorption. When you feel you are done, bring your hands together in prayer, salutation, or meditative *mudra* and complete your meditation with a moment of gratitude, reflection, or prayer to seal the energy of your meditation. Transmit the energy of that inner smile through your outer smile to everyone you meet.

Your own inner smile will be reflected back at you as a smile from everyone around you. The inner smile and outer smile are contagious. You can cultivate the inner smile anytime throughout the day and fill your heart with compassion and love for others, and you can smile an inner smile for the hearts of everyone around you.

The inner smile makes you very aware of and sensitive to your internal body and your inner self. Inner energy awareness is increased by doing the inner smile. It is vital to your progress in all practices and activities in life.

Make the inner smile the foundation of your prayer life or your meditation, or take simple inner smile breaks during the day. It's important to take your attention inward, away from the world of sensory bombardment. Feel your body.

When you learn to smile inwardly to the organs and glands, your whole body will feel loved and appreciated. It will counteract stress and tension and increase the flow of energy, or *qi*, from within and from the universe.

How can something so simple be so powerful? "The Inner Smile," by yoga teacher Lilias Folan, can be purchased on audiotape or CD from the Relaxation Company at relaxco@aol.com. Lilias is a world-renowned yoga teacher and her presentation is a very accessible and simple way to get the feeling of the inner smile, although you don't have to do yoga to achieve it. Taoist inner smile meditation is coupled with what is called the Golden Light Body, which is the energetic body representing the actual photonic or light body. The more we visualize this in the inner smile, the more we interact with the feeling of goodness, and the easier we find it to recognize that the light body, or the body of consciousness described using quantum physics, actually exists.

This is not simply an Oriental or Buddhist realization; every cell in our bodies is made up of millions of atoms and molecules and subatomic particles, all of which are made up of photons. Thus, this Golden Light Body is a reality. The inner smile and the Golden Light Body of Taoist *qi* teachings, also referred to as the energy body, are standard throughout all religions and all metaphysical teachings, and ultimately they are being discovered in scientific teachings. This is not something esoteric or sectarian.

Einstein's classic formula, $E = mc^2$, states that energy (E) is equal to the mass of an object (M) times the speed of light (C) squared. Thus, the physical body has a tremendous amount of energy potential, whether it is in the form of the Golden Light Body or any other form of potential energy where the amount of energy can be calculated from the mass of the body multiplied by the speed of light squared.

Ancient teachers developed an energy anatomy of the human body that recognized an inner heart of the inner heart, much as we have a third eye. This is beyond the emotional heart and the physical heart. The inner heart of the inner heart is directly connected to what we experience as the soul, a concept that has eluded definition in the West and still is not fully accepted by the Western scientific community.

There is a very specific route mapped through the inner heart and the inner self to the higher self and to the soul, and that route is found by following the inner smile. It really doesn't matter whether you make your inner smile part of a formal meditation or just simply remember to smile to yourself and to others. Nothing rigid stays alive, concepts included.

☼

"If you saw the film *Apollo 13* about my challenge during the re-entry on the Apollo 13 mission to the moon—you saw how we safely landed the spacecraft, and I can guarantee that I had a giant smile on my face. When the ship picked us up and we emerged from the capsule onto the deck, the whole ship was one big smile! I can also say that the whole world that was watching anxiously was one big smile when we came through it alive. How could we not smile? Great and good feelings always bring a smile like this. You always get a response with a smile.

"'Smile and the world smiles with you' is a powerful and well-known fact. Not a theory. Smiles also open up the door to friendly negotiations in every field where conflict resolution is an issue. I have seen it first hand."

—*Captain James Lovell*, U.S. Navy
Apollo 13 moon landing for NASA

Universal Language

by Elan Sun Star

"So many languages in the world,
and a smile speaks them all."
—*Dr. Sue*

A smile, like a picture, is a universal language that transcends not only every cultural boundaries but also every conceptual boundary. No matter what village or town or city you go to, a smile means the same thing regardless of your age, culture, ethnicity, financial status, faith, or nationality. A smile is a smile is a smile, and a smile by any other name looks the same. It comes from the heart; thus there are no misinterpretations. Innately, we know that we are all in this world together, and by smiling, we can unleash powerful forces from within.

For many years, I traveled the world as a photographer, journalist, painter, and musician, and I have been touched by the gracious, loving, heartwarming smiles offered to me in every country I've visited, be it the Canary Islands, Germany, France, England, the countries of Central and South America, Mexico, the United States, or Canada.

Wherever you travel, a smile is the currency that will buy you whatever you need. When you smile, it circles the world. There are so many languages in the world, and a smile speaks them all!

Research and clinical data related to the heart as an organ of perception shows that the heart, rather than the brain, is the main organ in the body for organizing and distributing information. Research demonstrates that smiling could be the most powerful thing you can do. And throughout this research, you'll find that there is nothing else in the world that can cost so little but mean so much for so many, including you!

"Smiles are contagious; be a carrier!"

A smile is the breath of the soul and the spirit revealed, painted upon the face for all to see, transcending space and time. A smile has a very rich and deeply empowering value that speaks the language of eternity and unity.

A smile will enhance your life, body, mind, and spirit, and do the same for those around you. You can inspire every-one with a smile. It is truly the spirit of GOD in action, the spirit of your own soul saying, "Give to yourself and give to others, and you will immediately receive in turn the gratitude from your own heart and from those around you."

"A good world starts with nothing less than a smile!"

A world filled with happiness, goodness, joy, and uplifting thoughts and feelings begins with a smile. You know the value of a smile. How many things, other than breathing, are so common to each person's needs and desires? What besides breathing and drinking water can equate to the power of a smile? A smile is free! You can give a smile to yourself and you can give it to others for free.

"A smile is a powerful weapon. You can even break ice with it."

In negotiations, a smile is the quickest way to an agreement. A frown equals no, and a smile equals *yes*! A great way to shortcut peace negotiations, mediation, or conflict resolution is by giving an authentic smile— the Duchenne smile, as it is called (more on this later)— smiling with your lips, with your eyes, and with your heart, and meaning it. Despite linguistic and national differences, the smile gets through. It speaks to the heart rather than the mind. A frown says no; a smile says, "Yes, of course!"

Some people show their most authentic smiles of acceptance and love by actually weeping while smiling— smiling and weeping for joy, a mixture of crying and smiling. Something touches their inner feelings and causes them to weep with joy.

"A smile of encouragement at the right moment may act like sunlight on a closed-up flower; it may be the turning point for a struggling life."

Smiling is a simple, effective, and universal way to communicate with yourself internally, as well as a way to communicate externally with those you meet in life. Communicate your joy, your happiness, your abundance, your generosity, and your appreciation for life, all of which will return and affect you beneficially on all levels—mental, emotional, and physical. A smile will take you the extra mile.

"What sunshine is to flowers, smiles are to humanity. They are trifles, to be sure; but scattered along life's pathway, the good they do is inconceivable."

Some people have lost their smiles. Share yours with them. Since a smile costs nothing and brings such great returns, isn't it worth it? Smile. Send out a good vibe and it will bounce back to you. Those who spread joy, happiness, and smiles cannot help but reap the rewards of smiling—happiness and joy coming back at you from others.

A smile enriches those who receive it, without making those who give it any poorer. It takes but a moment to smile, but the memory of a smile sometimes lasts forever. No one is so rich or mighty that they cannot get along without it, and no one is so poor that they cannot be made rich by it.

Yet a smile cannot be bought, begged, borrowed, or stolen, for it is something that is of no value to anyone until it is given away.

Some people are too tired to give you a smile. Give them one of yours, as no one needs a smile so much as he who has nothing left to give.

The smile signals to your own heart and mind that everything is okay—that you can relax and create a better world from right inside you, from your heart and on your face. It shouts to the world that your intentions are wholesome, good, and trustworthy.

"A smile is the levity and flying upward to Heaven balanced by the gravity and the grounding and the roots of the earth."

Perhaps you recall a time in your life when a smile and a kind word meant the world to you. Remember deeply how a smile brought you something you wanted and needed. Smile at your heart if your heart is anxious. Use this smile as you would a wholesome natural medicine, for, indeed, laughter is the best medicine.

Put on a happy face!

"A smile is the light in the window of the soul...indicating that the heart is at home."

Nineteenth-century scientists were obsessed with the human head and face. They measured skulls and tried to correlate brain size with ability. Phrenologists tried to predict human characteristics from the shapes of skulls. Criminologists tried to define the criminal face.

French neurologist Guillaume Duchenne mapped one hundred facial muscles in 1862. His work gave him insight into smiling. He pointed out that false or even half-hearted smiles involve only the muscles of the mouth, but the "sweet emotions of the soul" activate the *pars lateralis* muscles around the eyes.

In other words, authentic smiles activate muscles around the eyes, an action that crinkles the skin around the eyes. Since then, physiologists have talked about the

Duchenne marker in a smile—the crinkling crow's feet, a slight squint of the eyelids, along with a lift of the cheeks and the corners of your mouth. You know the signs. You recognize true delight in a friend's face.

**"The act of smiling is a gift that gives
a little piece of joy and sunshine
to brighten another's day."**

Psychologist Paul Ekman has gone back to the smile and found something very important: it can work in reverse. Dr. Ekman studied facial structure and smiling in both women and men and found that producing this Duchenne smile can bring about a sense of euphoria, happiness, joy, and genuine well-being.

The Duchenne smile, it seems, is accompanied by increased activity in the left prefrontal cortex, known to be the seat of positive emotions. What Ekman found is that you can activate your pleasure center by putting on a Duchenne smile.

Yes, you can literally make yourself happy by smiling!

We have been conditioned in our society to believe that a smile that does not come as an authentic Duchenne smile is absolutely cold and fake, but what we are finding is that we have the ability to recreate a state of happiness by recreating a smile.

When you have a simple formula for success, it is important to remember…repeat what works.

However, only spontaneity gives you the maximum result from a smile. A spontaneous smile activates far more synapses in your pleasure center than does a voluntary smile. So, you cannot fake happiness, but you *can create it* within yourself. And when you do, you deeply touch everyone around you.

That you can fake a smile and create happiness within yourself almost seems like a contradiction in terms. Of course, in life there are many instances where contradictory things are both true. Keep that in mind. You can personally practice what might be considered a fake smile even if you are not happy. By practicing the smile, you can actually activate the hormones and neurotransmitters to make yourself feel happy.

These are the remarkable results of research. The physiology of smiling creates a biochemical result. This is why it is best to "fake it till you make it" and act happy, even if it feels unnatural, no matter what anybody thinks—because when you start acting as though you're really smiling and really happy, you actually feel happier! It is somewhat like an actor taking on a role and totally giving him- or herself over to the character, finally *being* the character. And of course, this affects us whether we are optimistic or pessimistic in our general outlook on life. It affects our whole biochemistry.

In the past decades, extensive research has been done on facial expressions. In these studies, uncoached research subjects come in and make different facial expressions on cue. Of course, one of the expressions studied was a smile. It was found that smiling definitely increased the person's sense of well-being, health, and happiness, simply as a result of using the facial muscles to create a smile.

So, what do you do when you don't feel like smiling and you don't even feel like faking it? Well, you can be grateful that you're not being forced to smile, and that may make you smile! Remember, it is not mandatory to smile or to be happy!

The research behind the physiological effects of smiling is rigorous. Many motivational and inspirational teachers have based their teachings on these findings. Science says that you can actually use your physiology—in this case, smiling—to create a biochemical response, activating neurohormones, endorphins, and nitric oxide to make you feel great.

Success leaves clues. Think about it. What was the state you were in when you last felt happy? Well, go back to that state rather than trying to find an esoteric mental way to be happy. Smile until you're happy instead of thinking, "I wish I were happy so I could smile."

"Always remember to be happy, because you never know who's falling in love with your smile."

There are authentic smiles and inauthentic smiles, but we must also realize that there is an authentic *try* at being happy, and an authentic *try* at smiling.

So, maybe if you stand in front of the mirror and learn how to put on a Duchenne smile, you might develop those muscles around the eyes and forge that brain-mind connection so that the heart can take over and you can again feel joy, happiness, and love—just from smiling. Stop waiting for somebody else to change your life; stop waiting for a significant other to come into your life to make you happy. You don't even have to eat chocolate to be happy!

You can *smile* and be happy!

"Smiles are the soul's kisses."— *Minna Thomas Antrim*

A smile comes from one of the deepest places in the soul, and it was actually planted inside of you by that which created you and everything else in your universe. Maybe it is worth your time to wait for a smile to come spontaneously—but then again, your desire to create a smile and your desire to be proactively happy are also part of the spontaneous universe you live in.

So, whether you spontaneously pop a smile onto your face or whether you follow some of the protocols in this book—

- Smile for your health!
- Smile for your happiness and your joy!
- Smile for your abundance!
- Smile for the fact that nobody is telling you that you have to smile!

☼

"I travel around the world and from many people that I encounter, one of the most frequent questions that is asked is: 'If you were to choose a place to live or to visit next, where would you like for it to be?' Each time, I feel that it is not the place that makes it wonderful, but the smiling people that I meet in these places that I visit. The good energy and smiles that I receive from people when I visit places is what I remember the most. When I think about all the people that I have met, I wonder how many smiles I have encountered. No matter how beautiful the land is, if there are no smiles—I do not want to go, and vice versa.

"Smile and good HADO…this is what makes my work worthwhile, and I feel that I am contributing towards a more peaceful world."

—*Dr. Masaru Emoto*
Author of *The Hidden Messages in Water*
Featured in the film, *What the
Bleep Do We Know*

Rₓ for Happiness

by Elan Sun Star

"A SMILE is a facelift that's in
everyone's price range!"
—*Ziggy*

"The Face as Window and
Machine for the Emotions"
is the title of an article written by Dr. Robert Zajonc in
LSA Magazine. He is a clinical researcher and psycholo-
gist who researched the question, "Do we smile because
we are happy, or are we happy because we smile?" New
studies prove both to be true, says Dr. Zajonc. In other
words, you can create that state of happiness by faking
your smile.

Dr. William James, the psychologist from the turn of the
20th century and author of *As A Man Thinketh*, had a
more radical view about this. James was quite famous in
his time, and his books were top sellers throughout the
20th century. He is often quoted by leaders in the mind,
body, and spirit movement. James described the process
the other way around.

We always assume because of our social and emotional
conditioning that we smile because we are happy, and
we cry because we are sad, and we frown because we are
angry. According to Dr. James, it would be more rational

to say that we feel sorry because we cry, angry because we strike out at others, and afraid because we tremble, and not that we cry, strike, or tremble because we are sorry, angry, or fearful, as the case may be.

The body manifests emotion through a variety of muscles in the face and other parts of the body. That is exactly what smiling is.

Emotions also affect posture and movement. For example, when you are sad, your shoulders droop, your head is down, and your breathing is shallow. But when you are happy, you have that Duchenne smile, especially when your emotion is fully manifested in a physical expression. What research is showing is that when you simply fake it till you make it—when you stand up straight, inhale deeply, keep your chin up, and smile—you cannot be depressed. So it's very important to maintain the posture and attitude of a happy, empowered person.

These findings come from fields of study such as neurolinguistic programming (NLP) and psychoneuroimmunology, and from people such as the late Dr. Norman Cousins, who cured himself of bone cancer and other diseases by watching funny movies and constantly laughing and smiling, which elevated his endorphins and other immune system healers such as T-cells, lymphocytes, leucocytes, and phagocytes, which are brought into action to fight disease.

That is the importance of playing, laughing, and smiling. A gentle, heartfelt smile puts your biochemistry in the mental and emotional state of actually being happy, and once you see that it feels better than being angry or depressed, you generally stick with that feeling.

The face is a window to the emotions. Physiologists inherited from philosophers the assumption of a mind-body separation, a dualism that persists to this day. Aristotle's classic comment about dualism is, "Mental character is...conditioned by the state of the body, and contrary-wise, the body is influenced by the affections of the soul." Your mental and emotional states are affected by the state of your body, and the opposite is true—that your mental and emotional states affect the body. So, if you switch one, you will switch the other because there is a mind-body-spirit continuum.

You cannot underestimate the value of smiling. It helps you get to a state of real happiness—authentic and full of energy, playfulness, smiling, sharing, caring, hugging, joking, and humor. All of these things, along with being around naturally happy people, contribute to natural smiles. Learn how to transmute and transform situations through your own biochemistry and response. Transmute every situation into a happy one.

A spontaneous Duchenne smile is authentic, potent, and biochemically powerful in a therapeutic, healing situation, as well as being liberating and transformational. Inhaling and breathing and putting on as real a smile as you can affects your biochemistry. It can also heal you.

"A smile is medicine itself, and laughter is the best medicine."

Charles Darwin noted parallels between animals and humans in that there was uniformity in emotional expressions. Darwin was one of the first scientists to undertake a systematic study of this, published in his classic book, *The Expression of Emotions in Man and Animal*. He sent letters to thousands of people, including military men, government officials, missionaries, and friends who lived in distant parts of the British Empire, and asked them a series of very clear questions about whether the people in those areas expressed grief by weeping, joy by laughing, and openness by smiling.

The results of his survey led Darwin to accept the proposition of cross-cultural universal emotional expression in humans, no matter what culture or country they are from. Unfortunately, he did not know to ask his research subjects whether it was universal that smiling could make one happy. And they could have discovered whether the corollary was true—that if you cried, you could make yourself sad.

You can make yourself happy by putting on a smile, no matter what kind it is. Do your best. Sometimes it takes practice.

The face is a unique "organ" because it is externally displayed. You can see it in the mirror and other people can see it. It is not hidden; it is there for all to see. The face shows what is happening in the body, in the organs. There are systems of medicine over 5000 years old, such as Chinese and Ayurvedic medicine, in which disease is diagnosed in part by facial lines and wrinkles, and even by the iris in the eye. But can you reverse such a diagnosis?

The face is actually an instrument of social interaction, and it displays as much as, if not more about our emotions than, body language does. The muscles of the face are capable of countless expressions, and each movement has meanings for others. Many of those meanings are universal.

To paraphrase Gertrude Stein, a smile is a smile is a smile. If you observe people in conversations, you are likely to discover that it is not the exchange of knowledge and information that is important, but the expression and communication of emotions and feelings.

Dr. Zajonc says, "A common supposition globally is that the eyes are the windows of the soul and thus the best communicative message." Elsewhere, he says, "The very word 'expression' is in itself a theory, and could it be that we just don't feel an emotion and then express through the body, through the face, through the smile?" St. Jerome (A.D. 342–420) said, "The face is the mirror of the mind, and eyes without speaking confess the secrets of the heart."

Facial actions can precede and even cause feelings. A smile can change your feelings. In 1907, Israel Weinbaum, a Russian immigrant to France, wrote, "Facial gestures in general have regulatory and restorative functions for the vascular systems of the head." Dr. Zajonc noted that Weinbaum was onto something here. He observed that all emotional experiences produce considerable disequilibrium or change in the blood flow and vascular system, which supports Weinbaum's statement.

We smile to cool off our brains, just as we have a fan in a super-conductive computer to keep it cool. Smiling causes vascular dilation and increases blood flow to keep the brain cool, because the brain works within a very narrow range of temperatures. By increasing and facilitating the cooling process of the brain, smiling can alter the temperature of blood entering and leaving the brain, as well as communicating emotions to others.

What does "communicating emotions to others" mean? It means that when we smile, we invite others to share our space. A smile indicates that we are receptive and friendly, not hostile or attacking. It can also be an invitation to encounters and relationships. So smiling has an obvious social benefit.

A smile communicates a lot. And smiling triggers a cascade of neurohormones that affect our emotions. Smiling makes you feel good. Thus, laughter is the best medicine.

The brain cannot tolerate temperature variations as well as other organs. We depend on smiling to cool down the brain and keep it in that optimum range so that we feel good. The structure of the mouth and eyes when smiling can make us feel good by regulating our brain temperature, whether anybody is around or not.

So smile for yourself, too.

Dr. Zajonc states, "Because the metabolic activity of the brain requires continuous cooling, the absence of cooling of the brain is felt as discomfort and as a negative effect. Whereas increased cooling by smiling is felt as pleasurable and as a positive effect, and thus healing."

Other researchers explore the link between brain temperature and emotion in a different way. It turns out that metaphors like "hothead" and "boiling mad" and "cool as a cucumber" are not accidental.

Feelings are very kinesthetic. We can express them equally well in words or in facial expressions. Forehead temperature, a very good indicator of brain temperature, is higher for a person expressing anger than for one with a neutral expression, and definitely higher than for someone with a happy smiling face, which cools the brain.

Research shows that aggression, violence, and negative effects occur more readily when the brain temperature is high. Dr. Zajonc also stated, "Studied students gave an instructor more negative ratings when the classroom was on a high temperature than in a lower temperature."

Why do we scratch our heads when we are confused? There is a reason we rub our chins. Why do some people bite their fingernails, or chew on their pens or pencils? Why do people chew gum? Dr. Zajonc believes that these movements may help cool brain blood by moving cooled blood to the cavernous sinus in the skull more efficiently. In other words, these activities can help cool off the brain.

Thumb sucking may also be a prime example of this, but we don't suggest you do it if you're a grownup. Thumb sucking is a powerful unlearned action that is very hard to extinguish even after childhood. It forces nasal breathing that can cool the brain off quite quickly, and it also releases endorphins that have a pacifying effect. Smiling does the same thing. Try to make smiling a natural response, and it will make you happy and cool as a cucumber and keep you from being a hothead.

- A smile is health.
- A smile is joy.
- A smile is love.
- A smile says, "Hello, how are you?"
- A smile says, "We're on the same team."
- A smile says, "Let's create win-win and let's do this together!"

A smile can be your greatest tool in negotiations, in relationships, and elsewhere in your daily personal life. Don't underestimate its simplicity. By now it should be fairly obvious, but research and clinical data confirm that smiling is one of the simplest, most cost-effective therapies for whatever ails you.

Smile for your health; smile for your well-being; smile for your relationships. Together, we will create a world in which smiling is the key to happiness.

"As the conductor for the Moscow Chamber Orchestra and traveling around the world guest-conducting, I see that the human smile is enlivening, transforming and inspiring, just as the music I conduct and perform.

"In Russia and around the world, music and smiling are universal languages common to all cultures and people and to young and old alike. Music is the 'language of the soul,' your smile is a fine composition with the same ability to transform your spirit and your life.

"Smiling is a symphony/concerto of inspiring information and research that will make your heart sing. Just as the famed Stradivarius violins were crafted by a Master for exceptional, unparalleled abilities, so too an authentic smile can transform and entrance the world around you."

—*Constantine Orbelian*
**Conductor and Director,
Moscow Chamber Orchestra**

"Your smile is a gift to everyone, for as someone said, 'Everyone smiles in the same language.' From research we have conducted at the Institute of HeartMath, we know that a genuine smile, while shown on the face, emanates from the heart and is an expression of our complete inner and outer selves. Smiling many times a day should gladden everyone's heart—and thus lead to more smiles!"

—Rollin McCraty
Director of Research,
The Institute of HeartMath
www.heartmath.org

"What the Dalai Lama, Shirley Temple and Nelson Mandela and Joan Lunden already know, a smile is our inherent gift of happiness. Your bright smile is a wonderful reminder of what is so easily forgotten, yet so essential to life. Transformation and joy are simple and free."

—Luke Seaward, Ph.D.
Author of *Stand Like Mountain, Flow Like Water* and *Stressed Is Desserts Spelled Backward*

Spread It Around

by Elan Sun Star

"Be peace—smile."
—Buddhist monk *Thich Nhat Hanh*

Wherever you travel in the world, a smile is the currency that buys you just about anything you want, and it definitely buys you things you need. No matter where you travel, a smile means the same thing and it creates the same things—love, sharing, and communication.

Smiling is said to be the most important thing you can do, next to breathing. Since it doesn't cost you anything, why not smile authentically all day long? Everyone around you will love it. Have you ever noticed that the smiling, laughing people you meet attract you the most? They make you feel the best; they easily attract others. Everyone seems to listen to smiling people. Not so with frowning people.

A smile expands like a happy explosion. The energy of a smile ripples around the world like waves. You smile at two people, and they smile at two people, and so it goes. You might say a smile is like a *happy virus* that makes people feel good rather than bad, and there's no medicine that can cure a happy smile. It infects everybody; it makes a happy world. But why would you need a cure for a happy smile spreading around the world?

So, start a smile epidemic in your neighborhood today, and spread it to everyone you know! Maybe you'll hear the news report in the morning: "Smile virus detected in New York City; smile virus exploding in Los Angeles; smile virus spreading around the world," and there you'll be, smiling and giggling! Indeed, we hope there's no cure for the smiling virus, because it makes everyone feel happy.

The epidemic will explode in waves and ripples, and that wave will engulf everyone and cause them to smile. Within 24 hours, you will have reached every village, every town, every city, and every tribe in the world. You can't overestimate how quickly a smile can spread through the six degrees of separation.

Within every smile is the history of all good things that have ever happened to humanity and in the universe. This is not just hyperbole or metaphor. Is there any language that could convey what a smile does? How many millions of words would it take to express it?

A smile enriches immeasurably. Smiling only adds to; it never takes away from. A smile is God's way of saying everything's good. You just can't hide the joy in a smile. The best things in life are free, including smiles. Don't try to hide your smiles; it wouldn't work, anyway. Smiles are magical. The more you give them away, the more you have to give away. A smile isn't a smile if you hold on to it.

Whom would you rather be around—a smiling, happy person or a sad, frowning person? A smile can tell you everything you need to know about a person's character. It's all right there.

Smiles come in all shapes and sizes: shy smiles, bold smiles, enduring smiles, heartfelt smiles, laughing smiles, thoughtful smiles, gentle smiles, lots of teeth smiles, "I love you" smiles, "I know you do" smiles, smiles of gratitude, and smiles of agreement. No matter what shape, size, or strength, smiles always come from the heart.

A real, heartfelt smile is the best way to end a disagreement, an argument, a feud, or a war. A smile signs the bond of friendship. Sometimes it's even sealed with a hug or kiss. Smiles and hugs sometimes go together. They don't have to, but it's twice as good when they do. A smile is a facial handshake.

Nothing makes you prettier than a smile. Smiles can put plastic surgeons out of business. Only the cold and heartless fail to respond to a smile. A newborn, a baby, a child, or a 90-year-old person understands a smile. Even animals respond to smiles: golden retrievers are some of the best smilers.

A smile is not only a physical response of the facial muscles. What's really going on is a radiance of biophoton energy from the heart and from the center of one's being—mind, body, and spirit.

When tested in laboratories, the actual energy that goes with the smile is electromagnetic, radiant, extending through a field of energy that radiates outward from the body. We see a smile in the muscles of the face, in the relaxation of the body, and as an extension of warmth and energy.

If we were to photograph a smile using Kirlian photography and electromagnetic sensors, we would see that we are radiating like the sun when we smile. For most of us, we only feel the heart, we only see the face and the smile and the teeth. But what is really going on is radiant light, just like when we turn on the light switch.

But a smile is much, much, much, much more than even that. It's opening up your soul to everything around you and saying, "YES!" A smile is nothing less than YES! A real smile is the quickest way to get to total love.

A smile is naturally spontaneous. It floods forth from the depths of the soul. Who knows the enduring effect of a smile? Who knows how far a smile radiates into the universe?

Perhaps your smile is timeless, starting with you and going on for eternity. It's unlimited because it keeps spreading smiles, repeating its life-giving benevolence forever from one to another, from one to the many, from the many to all.

Smiling is so simple and inexpensive, with such profound health-giving and peace-bestowing effects, that it should be taught in schools. It should be taught to children; it should be taught in continuing education classes; it should be taught in trade schools and in colleges.

It should be taught to ambassadors throughout the world, to all consuls, to all diplomats. A smile is the best diplomatic introduction imaginable.

Smiles should be on the faces of police officers, school-teachers, professors, plumbers, clerks, farmers, husbands and wives, CEOs, and, yes, even politicians.

"Humble smile, you seem so small, your radiant joy does fill us all."

Smiling has been investigated as a medicine, as a potion, and as a healing agent. It has also been used as an extension of diplomatic well-wishing throughout history. From the beginning of time, a smile indicated a lack of hostility and a willingness to share and communicate.

Smiling has been studied extensively for over a century in both scientific and clinical research circles. Studies have looked at the biochemical and electrical effects of smiling, and the smile's health-giving effects on the human organism.

Smiling has even been shown to affect the growth of plants. Smiling at plants causes them to increase their growth and productivity, even to the point of increasing the number of flowers and fruits on trees. At the turn of the century, Luther Burbank, the well-known plant magician in what is now Burbank, California, created hundreds of varieties of fruits and vegetables by, among other things, smiling and loving his plants. It was a new form of genetic engineering: smiling and love.

New biology promoted by Bruce Lipton and other cell biologists demonstrates that our beliefs, thoughts, and feelings change our genetics, our RNA and DNA. We control our genes, not the other way around. We can see a loving smile change everything around us. The change goes far deeper than a smile's simple beneficial effect on negotiations—deeper than what can be effected by regulations, or even by cloning and other forms of genetic engineering. Responding with a smile to your perceptions, your emotions, and the world around you can change your whole reality. Now you know the truth.

Smiling is nothing less than pure, absolute magic. If I told you that smiling every day could change everything in your life for the better, would you believe?

BELIEVE ME!

When you're walking in nature, in a forest or through a meadow or across a beach, nature is smiling at you. When you're taking a shower, the water is smiling on you. When you're singing a song, every cell in your body is smiling along. When you're smiling on everyone, you can do no wrong.

The medical research establishment should have announced long ago that smiling is a cost-effective way to reduce blood pressure, obesity, and the risk of cancer, heart attacks, and other serious diseases. A smile and play keeps ill health away. Don't consult your doctor before administering a smile; just smile at ill health and laugh it away. If one smile is good, a thousand smiles a day is far better.

There are no contraindications or restrictions on smiling. You can never smile too much. You can never feel bad after smiling. In fact, you can never feel bad if you are smiling. It's a proven fact. Don't go to the library and look up the research to find out; just try it on your own.

If everyone in the world smiled, there would never be another war. Of course, the author believes that tourism and smiling people spreading the smiling virus around the world would bring peace much faster than peace negotiations. Those smiling faces are even spread around the world via e-mail attachments and other methods, spanning national and ethnic boundaries to show that people around the world smile in the same language.

E-mails of smiling faces, websites featuring smiling faces, and publications with smiling faces from around the world can be enlisted as carriers of this healthy, happy smiling virus.

Anyone who hasn't been prejudiced by cultural con-ditioning can help to spread a feeling of goodwill by smiling globally, smiling when they're traveling, smiling when they're vacationing, smiling when they're in a dif-ferent country, and smiling when they're at home, help-ing to spread this goodwill ambassadorship to the entire world. How is it that something so simple and effective could have been ignored for so long? Most likely because it is so simple.

If everyone in the world smiled, money would not be as important. Smiling is the best life insurance. The monthly payments are a lot less than what is demanded by your insurance company.

How many arguments have been prevented by smiling? How many feuds have been avoided with smiling? We will never know the exact number, but you can rest assured, the number is in the billions.

Think of everything beautiful as being a smile. Show your appreciation for beauty by smiling. Although we may have symbols of outward abundance, what would our world be without smiles? You could travel the world forever looking for riches and power, but what would life be like if you could never give or receive a smile?

Remember humor, laughter, joking, tickling, and playing. They all lead to cathartic, healing releases that can make you more intelligent, make you hardier and resistant to stress diseases, and definitely make you more fun to be around. That may be the most important thing. The more fun we are to be around, the more we share, and the more we share, the more we spread happiness and the smile virus around the world.

More sharing, more caring. Even the economy of the world increases as we share. I spend my capital and give it to you; you spend it and give it to 10 other people; they spend it and it goes to a thousand people; they spend it and it goes to millions; and thus, through the six degrees of separation and a shrinking globe, we've covered the whole world in less than a day. So it is with the smiling virus.

So spend your money. Share it. Be liberal. Manifest abundance. Economies increase when we spend and share. The increase spreads around the world. Hearts increase, health increases, and wisdom and joy increase when we smile. Remember, though, you don't have to work as hard for a smile as you do when you are working to earn money. Just let that smile come. It's free. It's the quickest way to buy what you want. It's the quickest way to talk to anybody in the world. And a smile is the real you: it's the true you.

Smile for wisdom and intelligence; smile for a new world. Remember—infect the world with the smiling virus. The epidemic will spread. No drug can stop it. Rejoice in that, because it's the ultimate virus—one that lets us ignore all the rest.

Try it. Smile at everybody you meet. Get them to laugh or smile. If they won't smile, use extreme measures. It may take serious measures to bring about an epidemic of smiling. You might have to tackle people and tickle them. You might have to hug them. Whatever measures are needed, go for it. Do whatever it takes.

Use a hug the same way you use the Heimlich maneuver. Grab the person from behind, hug them, tickle them, and make them laugh. It will get them to breathe again. It's much better than the Heimlich maneuver!

Whatever it takes, get people to smile. Find reasons to smile:

- Smile at people's wisdom.
- Smile at their generosity.
- Smile at their willingness to see your smile.
- Smile at all the things they do.
- Smile at their willingness to learn from their mistakes.
- Smile at the fact that God lives in them.
- Smile at people because they're beautiful.

- Smile at people because they're trying.
- Smile at people because God created them.
- Smile at people, or smile at nature.
- Smile at yourself.
- Smile in your heart.
- Smile at your heart.
- Smile to your liver, to your kidneys, to your lungs, and to your spleen.
- Smile to the ocean.
- Smile to the mountains.
- Smile to the trees.
- Smile to the flowers.
- Smile to the birds.

Smile at everything. Make it an automatic reaction. Make it authentic. The more you practice a smile, the easier it becomes. Think of the smile as a muscle you can increase with practice. It will make your heart stronger, too.

☼

"Smiling at others is very uplifting!

"This knowledge comes at a time when life is full of pain and anguish. Smiles are good for the heart and for peace. Inner peace and world peace. It is essential for everyone to spread the smiles far and wide around the world."

—*Arun Gandhi*
Founder/President, *Mahatma Gandhi Institute for Nonviolence*—an organization to strengthen and co-create global peace
Grandson of Mahatma Gandhi

"Smiling is an innate response to feeling good, as crying is to feeling bad."

—*David Chamberlain, Ph.D.*
Author, *The Mind of Your Newborn Baby*
Association for Prenatal &
Perinatal Psychology

Refresh the Spirit

by Patricia Bragg, N.D., Ph.D.

 In my lifetime of travel-ing the world I have been everywhere and seen every-thing, and I can tell you that I know that the human smile and what it brings is priceless for us all!

Since I have traveled around the world 13 times, spoken and been on radio and television thousands of times in the past 55 years, I know a lot about human psychology, and I can tell you that there is nothing as healthy as a smile to refresh the spirit and the heart of anyone you meet.

And if you meet someone without a smile, please give them one of your own…they will most often pass it on.

My dad, Paul C. Bragg, who was known for his smile, was the father of the health movement and originator of health food stores. He inspired millions to live a healthy lifestyle with the Bragg Crusades and Bragg Health Books worldwide.

Everyday he woke up with a smile and went to bed with a smile. He loved life, and he had *agape* love for everyone!

The smiles we give and receive daily are so powerful! Your smile is powerful because it is instantly effective to bring a healthy welcome to all receiving your smiles.

Wherever I go, throughout the world, smiles are so important. Whether I'm at the Beach Boys' homes, Clint Eastwood's, Steve Jobs', or the United States White House, I feel my smile gives a welcome from my spirit and mind and heart to all I greet!

Successful people have one thing in common: they all know and respect the power of their smiles and the smiles in their lives. We all know from a lifetime of personal experience that a smile is our greatest and best asset!!

* * * * *

Patricia Bragg, Ph.D., is a health and lifestyle educator to world leaders, Hollywood stars, American business giants, U.S. Presidents, and champion athletes

☼

"Smiling is something we all need to do. I have seen it work miracles. At the Institute of Noetic Sciences that I founded many years ago, soon after my space flights, we pioneer research into the mysteries of life and the science-based paradigm."

—*Edgar Mitchell*, Astronaut
Founder, *Institute of Noetic Sciences*

A Smile Saves an Author's Life:
Antoine de Saint-Exupery

by Elan Sun Star

The Little Prince is a well known and lovely book by Antoine de Saint-Exupery.

The Little Prince is famous around the world and has sold millions of copies in its lifetime and inspired many a child, parent or seeker. Very few who have read this mystical book know that Saint-Exupery was a fighter pilot who fought against the Nazis and was killed in action. Before World War II, he fought in the Spanish Civil War against the fascists and had many close encounters with death.

Antoine wrote a beautiful story based on some of these experiences, entitled **The Smile** (*Le Sourire*).

Antoine said that he was captured by the enemy and thrown into a jail cell with little hope of escaping. Judging by the dangerous looks and nasty treatment he received from his jailers, he would be executed sooner than later.

Here is what Saint-Exupery wrote in this story of the power of a Smile to rescue one from death:

* * * * *

"I was sure that I was to be killed. I became terribly nervous and distraught. I fumbled in my pockets to see if there were any cigarettes which had escaped their search. I found one and, because of my shaking hands, I could barely get it to my lips.

"But I had no matches, they had taken those. I looked through the bars at my jailer. He did not make eye contact with me. After all, one does not make eye contact with a thing, a corpse. I called out to him, 'Have you got a light, por favor?' He looked at me, shrugged and came over to light my cigarette. As he came close and lit the match, his eyes inadvertently locked with mine. At that moment, **I smiled**. I don't know why I did that.

"Perhaps it was nervousness, perhaps it was because, when you get very close, one to another, it is very hard not to **smile**. In any case, **I smiled**. In that instant, it was as though a spark jumped across the gap between our two hearts, our two human souls. I know he didn't want to, but **my smile leaped through the bars** and generated a **smile on his lips, too**.

"He lit my cigarette but stayed near, looking at me directly in the eyes and continuing to **smile**. I **kept smiling** at him, now aware of him as a person and not just a jailer. And his looking at me seemed to have a new dimension, too.

"'Do you have kids?' he asked.

"'Yes, here, here.' I took out my wallet and nervously fumbled for the pictures of my family. He, too, took out the pictures of his niños and began to talk about his plans and hopes for them.

"My eyes filled with tears. I said that I feared that I'd never see my family again, never have the chance to see them grow up. Tears came to his eyes, too. Suddenly, without another word, he unlocked my cell and silently led me out.

"Out of the jail, quietly and by back routes, out of the town. There, at the edge of town, he released me. And without another word, he turned back toward the town.

"My life was saved by a smile. Yes, the smile—the unaffected, unplanned natural connection between people.

"I tell this story in my work because I'd like people to consider that underneath all the layers we construct to protect ourselves, our dignity, our titles, our degrees, our status and our need to be seen in certain ways—underneath all that, remains the authentic, essential self. I'm not afraid to call it the soul."

* * * * *

Antoine de Saint-Exupery's story speaks of that miraculous moment when two souls recognize each other, and the **smile** is the main contributing factor to transformation.

This story reveals one more of the infinite examples of true stories of people's lives that were dramatically and beneficially changed for the better by a single yet powerful bonding smile of recognition—recognition for the higher part of the soul and beyond conflicts and momentary prejudices and barriers.

Smiling can even transform hate and rejection. You will only be able to know this fact when you test it out in your daily life.

You never know whose life you save with a smile. You can also be ready to accept and coax a smile out of a shy or scared person who just needs that one little gesture to unlock their potential to expand and grow in life in a magical way…

☼

"It's been said that everyone smiles in the same language. And it's true. Smiling not only makes us and others feel good, it also bridges across the divides that can make us feel isolated. Smiling is not only a step toward health and happiness, but a step toward world peace. Your genuine smile can transform lives beginning with your own. I have seen this through my travels and talks."

—John Robbins
Author of *Healthy at 100,*
***Diet For A New America*, and**
The Food Revolution

Smiling 101

by Elan Sun Star

"If you have made another person on this earth smile, your life has been worthwhile."
—Sr. Mary Christelle Macaluso

Now you have some idea of the power of a simple smile. Remember that by spreading this beneficial expression to everyone you know, and even to those you've never met, you can affect the state of the world you live in with very little effort. You can affect your own feelings as well.

So, what do you do when you don't feel like smiling and don't even feel like faking it? Well, you can be grateful that you're not getting forced to smile, and that may make you smile. Remember, it is not mandatory to smile, nor is it mandatory for you to be happy.

Smiling Experiment!

Why not try a little experiment that takes very little time, no money, and very little effort on your part? Ask your friends and everyone you know whether they prefer being around a person who's smiling or frowning. Ask yourself the same question. Ask yourself whom you gravitate to at a party or gathering—the people who are exuding smiles and happiness or those who seem angry or depressed? The answer, in most cases, is obvious.

You don't have to cultivate a spiritual practice or take a course in self-improvement or how to influence others, nor do you have to take a course in socio-biochemical agreement-producing behaviors. A smile comes from a much deeper place. And it was actually planted there, deep inside, by that which created you and everything else in your universe.

Maybe it's worth waiting for a smile to come spontaneously, but who's to say that trying to create the smile by faking it until it feels good is not part of the spontaneous universe you live in? So, whether a smile spontaneously lights your face or whether you follow some of the protocols of this book—

- Smile for your health!
- Smile for your happiness and joy!
- Smile for your abundance!
- Smile for the fact that nobody is telling you that you have to smile!

But, for whatever reason you decide to smile, share that good feeling with those around you. They cannot help but smile right back! All too often in life, we realize that complex and expensive status symbols are nowhere near as potent and life-giving as the good things that are free.

Smiling is certainly one of those things!

It is free and effortless, and it brings immediate results. If people don't smile back at you, they probably need the smile more than anybody. So don't judge them because they don't have smiles, or because they're not sharing their smiles with you. Maybe they really need your smile to provide them with a seed that will grow into their own smiles.

They will remember the good feeling your smile brought them, and when they're feeling a little better, they might give it back to you or to someone else quite spontaneously. They just might pass it along.

And remember, also, that when you don't feel like smiling, you don't have to. But it's okay for you to gravitate toward people who are smiling and laughing. It will make your burden a lot lighter.

Laughter, humor, and, most of all, smiling, make us feel at home no matter how down or negative we might be feeling.

So, you are not obliged to be smiling all the time. There is no punishment for not smiling, and no reward for smiling except the state of feeling good and being around those who feel good, which in turn makes you feel even better.

A smile is a good cure for whatever ails you. Whether you're interested in handling a chronic disease, curing an acute disease, or managing pain; whether you're involved with emotional challenges, financial challenges, or relationship challenges; whether you're seeking optimum health and well-being for yourself or seeking to bring someone else a unique gift, a smile is always a good way to bring about your desired goal.

At times, you may think it is inappropriate to smile because the challenges in the world are too serious, or a critical situation demands a serious face. When you feel committed to transcending suffering, remember this: nothing soothes pain better than a smile.

A gentle smile may be more appropriate than a broad smile in some situations. Let the appropriate smiling response come from your heart. It will quickly bypass any cultural, conceptual, or philosophical differences and go straight to the heart of the other person.

Smiling is needed the most when challenges are the greatest. A smile reassures the heart that all things will pass, that challenges will be transcended and healed in time. On a happier note, a smile is very much like a boomerang: it always comes back to the sender. And just as with e-mail, if you send out smiles over the world-wide web of life, you'll get a notification that the smiles were received. There are already "National Smile Days"!

Let's make a "Global Smiling Day" when the celebration and festivities manifest in smiles encompass the entire globe. As in the saying, "Let peace begin with me," you can say, "Let peace begin with a smile, and let the smiling begin with me." It is an assurance that there is only good will.

- A smile is immediate!
- A smile is now!
- A smile is free!
- A smile is powerful!
- A smile is complete in itself!
- A smile is goodwill itself!

 A smile doesn't require any other gift, but you can always add a smile to any gift you give. In fact, it is the greatest gift you can give, and you can give it frequently. You can never give or receive too many smiles. You can vary the intensity of each smile and let your heart give each smile a definite purpose, a definite well-wish.

Those who receive your smile will know its profound meaning with no need for an interpreter.

When you feel least inclined to smile, smile anyway! It is a good affirmation to your mind, body, and spirit. It'll remind you that things will get better.

☼

"Everytime you smile at someone, it is an action of love, a gift to that person, a beautiful thing."

—Mother Teresa **(1910–1998)**

Five Things Your Smile Tells Others About You

by Elan Sun Star

A while back, I talked about what's in a smile, and I'd like to revisit those thoughts because smiling is such a great way to create positivity in your days.

- Sensitivity
- Maturity
- Insurance
- Leverage
- Emotion

These are some of the things one can find in a smile.

Sensitivity—When you smile at someone, you are conveying a number of things. Several of them I'm going to expand on here. For **S**, I have chosen Sensitivity. A smile lets the person you are conversing with know that you are sensitive and in tune with what they are saying.

Maturity—Smiling conveys a sense of maturity because if you can smile at times when you least feel the desire to smile, you show maturity and growth as a person. You are letting people know that even in the hard times, you value a positive attitude above the irrational.

Insurance—A warm smile tells people that you value them and that you are in fact listening to what they have to say. So, smile and be genuinely interested in the people around you.

Leverage—Leverage sounds a bit manipulative, but I don't mean it in that sense. A smile makes you much more approachable, and therefore you are more likable. If closer relationships with your family or the people you work with are what you desire, try smiling more openly.

Emotion—Last, but definitely not least, your smile conveys love. Everyone likes to feel loved and can use more of it in their lives. So, love them with your smile.

Believe it or not, a smile takes less effort to wear than a frown, so save yourself the energy and smile often.

The benefits of having the smile returned and the positives of a warm attitude are well worth it.

Part 2

Everyone Is Smiling

The following section includes contributions from and conversations with others who have furthered the research into the smile. Their contributions of time and effort are much appreciated, and bring a big smile to my face. Hopefully, they will bring a smile to your face as well.

—*Elan Sun Star*

Healing

I love my friends!
I want more friends.
I love Smiles.
That is a fact.

How to develop Smiles…
There are a variety of Smiles.
Some smiles are sarcastic.
Some smiles are artificial and diplomatic smiles.
These smiles do not produce satisfaction and Happiness.
A genuine loving smile gives us hope and
health and freshness.
If we want a genuine Smile, then first we
must produce the basis for a Smile to come.
Your Smile will bring healing to others and yourself.

—Tenzin Gyatso
His Holiness the 14th Dalai Lama
Head of state and spiritual leader
of the Tibetan people

☼

The Institute of HeartMath®: Rollin McCraty, Ph.D.

by Elan Sun Star

New research from the fields of psychophysiology and neurocardiology reveals that the heart is a principal organizing and information-dispersing center in the body and is also intimately involved in our emotional experience.

While the heart has long been associated with spiritual influx, wisdom, and positive emotions such as love, compassion, and appreciation, new research findings are now providing evidence that these associations may be more than merely metaphorical.

The Institute of HeartMath in Boulder Creek, California, is conducting groundbreaking research looking at the heart as an intelligent system whose rhythmic patterns of activity influence the functioning of the brain and entire body—including our thoughts, feelings, and behavior. In particular, this research has uncovered an intriguing link between the heart and genuine positive emotions. Dr. Rollin McCraty, Ph.D., the Institute of HeartMath's Executive Vice President and Director of Research, explains exciting scientific findings on the heart's critical role in emotional experience:

"In the history of Western science, the study of physiology has focused to a great extent on the pathways by which the brain 'talks' to the body and thereby regulates the functioning of the body's many organs and systems. However, comparatively little attention has been given to the equally complex communication pathways by which the bodily organs 'talk' to the brain. There is extensive evidence that the information the body continuously sends the brain not only plays a homeostatic regulatory role, but also actually influences higher-order brain functions, including perception, cognition, and emotional processing."

In essence, the messages the body sends the brain affect how we perceive and respond to the world around us, and they also affect how we feel.

While all the major bodily organs communicate with the brain, the heart possesses an especially strong communication link, states Dr. McCraty. It is not widely known that there are actually more neural pathways carrying information from the heart to the brain than from the brain to the heart!

Another fact that most people don't realize is that, far more than a pump, the heart is actually a sophisticated information encoding and processing center. The nervous system within the heart, containing more than 40,000 neurons, is so complex that neuroscientists call it a "little brain" in its own right!

Dr. McCraty explains how the heart's rhythmic beating patterns, which change from moment to moment, have a lot to say about our emotional state. When we are feeling stress or negative emotions, the heart's rhythm becomes disordered and erratic, looking something like a range of jagged mountain peaks. This incoherent heart rhythm signals an "out-of-sync" psychophysiological state that puts stress on all the body's systems. However, when we smile and experience positive emotions, a dramatic shift occurs within the heart, causing its rhythm to become ordered and harmonious, resembling a smooth and orderly sine wave.

This shift in the heart rhythm is the key marker of a beneficial psychophysiological state that the Institute of HeartMath has termed *coherence*. The Institute's research over the past 15 years has shown that the coherent state facilitates the body's natural regenerative processes and is associated with a wide range of physiological and psychological health benefits. These include improved functioning of the nervous, cardiovascular, and hormonal systems, as well as increased emotional stability and improved cognitive performance.

There is even new evidence that increasing coherence may enhance the processes underlying intuition.

As the heart's rhythms change, so do the messages that the heart relays to the brain. As mentioned above, it's been discovered that these messages play a big role in determining the emotions we experience. When we smile, the heart produces a more harmonious, coherent rhythm and sends a message to the brain that signals we are "feeling good." This message from the heart to the brain actually reinforces and adds texture to our experience of positive emotions like appreciation, happiness, or love.

The brain also receives messages from other organs, including the 42 muscles that regulate our facial expressions. Thus, in the physical act of smiling, our facial muscles send a "feel-good" message to the brain. Like the heart's message, this signal from the facial muscles also helps to create and sustain positive emotions.

So, by smiling, you actually *change the pattern of information going from your body to your brain*. This has a big impact on health and well-being, both short-term and long-term. States Dr. McCraty,

"Research shows that the brain functions as a complex pattern-matching system. The messages it receives from the heart, facial muscles, and other bodily organs are some of the many input patterns that the brain is constantly processing. These patterns play a critical role in our experience of emotions. An important point is that as recurring patterns of input to the brain become familiar, the brain attempts to maintain these familiar patterns as a stable baseline or norm. This occurs even if a familiar pattern is one that is ultimately detrimental to our health and well-being.

This mechanism actually provides a psycho-physiological basis for understanding why chronic stress can be so difficult to change: the brain learns to recognize the stressful patterns as familiar, and thus attempts to maintain and reinforce them, even though they are unhealthy.

"However, just like resetting a thermostat, it is also possible to introduce a *new* set of patterns, which, by repetition, become familiar to the brain and become established as a new baseline. So, if we consciously make efforts to smile and activate positive emotions, eventually the brain will recognize these coherent, 'feeling-good' patterns as familiar and will reinforce *them*. These coherent patterns promote optimal functioning of the body's systems, thereby reducing stress, enhancing health and vitality, and also improving our performance in many areas.

"Once we establish increased coherence as a new 'baseline' pattern in our system, feelings of well-being—and smiles, too—become much more a part of our natural state—something we experience spontaneously and on a consistent basis in our lives. Having this new, healthy baseline pattern also makes it a lot easier to 'bounce back' when we do experience stress or challenge. That's what the HeartMath coherence-building tools and techniques are about—they're designed to help you learn how to activate and hold heart-centered positive emotional states—a 'heart smile' if you will—so that you are able to intentionally create and sustain the many beneficial effects of smiling and experiencing positive emotions."

* * * * *

But the powerful effects of smiling don't just stop within our own bodies. They also radiate out into our environment, influencing other people around us. Institute of HeartMath research is showing that the electromagnetic field generated by the heart is central to this process.

The heart generates by far the strongest rhythmic electromagnetic field produced by the body, Dr. McCraty explains. This field surrounds us and can be measured several feet away from the body.

Furthermore, the information within the heart's field changes as we experience different emotions. When we smile and feel positive emotions, as the heart's rhythms become more coherent, the heart's electromagnetic field becomes correspondingly more organized.

"What is even more exciting is that our research is showing that our heart's field is actually registered physiologically by people around us—even influencing their brain activity!

This means that our heart's field has a very real effect on others in our environment. And because the heart's field changes dynamically with our emotions, this provides a physiological mechanism by which our emotional states influence those around us.

"So when we choose to smile and consciously activate positive emotions, our heart's field electromagnetically transmits that coherent, harmonious information into our environment, where it affects other people.

Research also shows that animals—and plants, too—are sensitive to and respond to the information contained in these electromagnetic signals.

As more people in a given environment activate a 'heart smile,' with feelings of appreciation, gratitude, love, or deep care, the effect becomes even more powerful. In effect, we're literally transforming our environment as we smile!"

So next time there's a smile on your face—and next time you consciously *choose* to bring a smile to your day and someone else's—take a moment to reflect on its far-reaching effects. Concludes Dr. McCraty:

"The science shows that by consciously cultivating a smile—both on your face and in your heart—you can take a proactive role in creating your own health, happiness, and fulfillment, while positively affecting others and your environment."

Now, that's *really* something to smile about!

* * * * *

Resources:
For more information on the Institute of HeartMath's research, programs, and coherence-building tools, visit their website at www.heartmath.org.

Scientific e-books available on the Institute of HeartMath's website:

- *The Appreciative Heart: The Psycho-physiology of Positive Emotions and Optimal Functioning*—Find out more about the physiology of positive emotions and the beneficial state called "coherence," and learn two HeartMath techniques to help you generate this state at will.
- *Heart-Brain Neurodynamics: The Making of Emotions*—More detail about the brain's pattern-matching function and the heart's important role in emotional experience.
- *The Energetic Heart: Bioelectromagnetic Interactions Within and Between People*—Discover how your heart's electromagnetic field and your emotions affect people around you!
- Add a smile to your day with uplifting Heart Quotes, delivered to your e-mail box Monday through Friday—a free service offered by HeartMath. To sign up, go to www.heartmath.com/free_services.html

"Smiling is spiritual medicine. I always tell people who come to pray in my synagogue that it doesn't matter if they know the words or melodies, as long as they keep a smile on their face as they seek to access the Divine. The joyous spiritual energy of the universe is *God's Smile*—and as long as we smile, we open the gates of heaven and connect to God's love. Keep smiling!"

—*Rabbi Michael Lerner*
www.tikkun.org/rabbi_lerner
Editor, *Tikkun Magazine*
Chair, Network of Spiritual Progressives
www.spiritualprogressives.org

Smiling From the Eyes

by Win Wenger, Ph.D.

"From Picasso's *Guernica* on, the visual arts of the 20th Century appeared mostly dedicated to portraying the deepest horrors of human experience around the planet. Offsetting that almost single-handedly is the timeless power of the human smile, especially 'smiling from the eyes.' Smiles are an optimistic trend."
—*Win Wenger, Ph.D.*

Smiling with your eyes as well as your mouth is the key to powerful smiling. It is the eyes that make the real smile the tremendous thing that it is.

In my book, *The Einstein Factor*, and in other books and papers, I refer to *Borrowed Genius*—a procedure that uses patterns of body feeling to direct the limbic brain (primarily the amygdala) to instruct the cortex on how to handle a given stimulus.

This feeling state can be quite important when responding to any event in order to do so in an optimum state of coherence and emotional and physical awareness.

Our body patterns govern intellectual responses, and the physical states that we are in dramatically affect our states of mind and responses.

When you are smiling and your eyes are in a sense lifting up the corners of your mouth, this is an optimum physiological state to produce results. Please note: Smiling with the lip muscles alone does not produce this effect, but smiling with the muscles around the eyes does. You need both eyes and mouth smiling to gain the maximum benefits.

The research in this area of smiling can be verified by reading the papers and clinical data available online and in libraries, but suffice it to say that smiling produces dramatic effects on one's state of mind, emotions, and physiology, and they co-create a state of optimum response to any challenge, demand, or request.

Why is smiling so important for us to be at our best and to access the greater realm of intellect and real genius? This is much of what I teach in my books and papers, which you can access from the educational links on my website, www.winwenger.com.

Information for solving issues and meeting creative demands is more readily accessible to the conscious mind when you achieve certain states of physiology. I use a technique called *Velvety-Smooth Breathing* to create this state of physiological non-stress so that the higher functions of the brain/mind continuum are allowed to enter the equation, and this affects the mind and body much as smiling does.

With simple additions to your basic physical posture and breathing tempo, you can dramatically affect your intelligence—both IQ and EQ (Emotional Intelligence).

There is another aspect of smiling that can also enhance your beneficial state, and that is increasing your access to information other than logical or conditioned conscious information.

The information that most of the public accesses is limited to a tiny percentage of the total available data for answering any question, dilemma, or challenge.

Why is it that we access so little of this intelligence potential? The answer is quite obvious if you are willing to look at it without prejudice.

We are in such a state of urgent demand, emotional stress, or acting out of conditioned social responses that we have only conditioned limited responses or the Robot Factor. Furthermore, we have a lifetime accumulation of decisions made under such pressures, which, when re-examined with greater maturity and more informed judgment, might prove to be no longer appropriate.

When we check out of consensus reality long enough to allow the bigger picture, the higher state of mind and body and consciousness, to operate, we are led to literal miracle solutions.

Simple as it might seem, smiling from the eyes is one of these techniques. And yet, more than a posed technique, it is a built-in hardwired response that is common to and functional in all cultures. It is a universal language of sorts, a Rosetta Stone of emotional introductions for all cultures.

I have witnessed and researched dramatic improvements in IQ and/or apparent intelligence from using certain simple techniques, which I teach in my books and in papers you can access freely online at www.winwenger.com.

What you do affects your brain and intelligence. There are few things as simple as smiling from the eyes that can complement and supplement these techniques to increase their combined effectiveness in increasing your intelligence and your overall well-being.

By creating a state conducive to reduced stress and breathing alterations and smiling, we can create a super state of receptivity to the bigger picture and the specific solution at the same time. You can find references to these techniques at my website, www.winwenger.com.

What smiling accomplishes, in my opinion, is a synthesis.

Smiling from the eyes allows a relaxed and visualizing brain to accomplish many miraculous tasks with no effort. You can experiment with the effect yourself:

Try smiling from the eyes, even without lip muscles; compare the internal effects of that to smiling with lip muscles only, without involvement from the eyes.

The reason smiling from the eyes is unique is that it is already practiced in all cultures with little restraint, if not inhibited by social strictures, rules, personal self-consciousness, or shyness.

This is part of the unique power of the smiling response, and it increases human potential on many levels—in other words, it brings about optimum and full functioning on all levels.

Smiling is contagious, and the good feelings it spreads to others are reflected on their faces as they respond. It charges the emotional field with positive energy, and we all have an inexhaustible supply. No matter how complex the scholarly theory of its physiology, it's that simple in practice. So do it every chance you get.

* * * * *

About Win Wenger:

Win Wenger, Ph.D., is a pioneer in the fields of creativity and creative method, accelerated learning, brain and mind development, and political economy. Formerly a college teacher, Dr. Wenger is a world-renowned trainer and the author of 48 published books, including his breakthrough text of techniques to facilitate scientific discovery and technical invention, *Discovering the Obvious*, and the popular bestseller, *The Einstein Factor.* Visit his website, www.winwenger.com

"The human smile is a necessity in a world of hostility, selfishness and alienation. A smile can change a face, a state of mind, a life, opening the gates to the simplicity of joy. We have a choice to sink into the fathoms of negativity or simply open our hearts and let love lead the way. Your smile is a necessary counter-balancing force to the dark messages we daily receive from newspapers and television and media. Smiling can uplift and inspire."

—*Xanya Sofra-Weiss, Ph.D.*
Neurophysiologist and Clinical
Psychologist, Author

"Simple. Clear. Refreshing. Illuminating. Uplifting. Stimulating. Sincere. Relevant. Practical. True. Smiling is powerful and free. Be sure to smile and let it touch you. It will make your day."

—*Alan Cohen*
Author of *A Deep Breath of Life*; *Relax Into Wealth*; *The Dragon Doesn't Live Here Any More*; *I Had It All the Time*; *Dare To Be Yourself*.
www.alancohen.com

Positive Emotions:
Barbara Fredrickson, Ph.D.

by Elan Sun Star

"Genuine smiles reflect perhaps the most crucial renewable human resource of our times—positive emotions. As they accumulate and compound, genuine smiles and heartfelt positive emotions transform people and communities for the better. You can hardly prevent yourself from being moved and transformed by the beauty, joy and hope created by the simple act of smiling."
—*Barbara Fredrickson, Ph.D.*

Dr. Barbara Fredrickson is with the Department of Psychology at the University of Michigan. Her work on positive emotions has won many awards. She also won the top prize ever awarded by the John Templeton Foundation, the Positive Psychology Award, a $100,000 award for the best research to date in positive psychology and positive emotions. This is an incredible testimony to Dr. Fredrickson's work and papers published on positive psychology and positive emotions, as well as her work with other psychologists and other researchers.

Through the John Templeton Foundation, Dr. Templeton uses his vast resources to develop the fields of positive psychology, astronomy, medicine, and biochemistry in order to demonstrate that creation mirrors our human abilities to create and extend a beneficent feeling of well-being and healing, health and wholesomeness in the world. This creativity is furthered through positive psychology and activities such as smiling.

Dr. Fredrickson's work is so astoundingly good that it is tempting to divert from the specific arena of smiling to talk about positive emotions and how they benefit humans in all aspects of their lives and relationships. But I will continue with some information that Dr. Fredrickson has shared with me regarding research on smiling and the benefits that authentic smiling bestows upon the smiler and the smilee.

Although I will restate here that even a fake smile can jumpstart the beneficial flow of endorphins and good-feeling biochemistry, we return to the authentic Duchenne smile and why it is important to develop the authentic smile in one's own physiology. It only takes a little bit of training to detect the Duchenne smile in oneself and in others. Dr. Fredrickson's work shows that an authentic smile indicates a person's willingness to be receptive to the environment, to learning, to taking in new information, and to dialogue and discussion.

This openness can be used in peace negotiations, where an authentic smile breeds an environment of receptiveness and willingness to learn, rather than insisting on negotiating from a position of power without regard for the information being shared by the other side.

Of course this assumes an authentic Duchenne smile, a smile that involves the *orbicularis oculi* around the eyes and the *zygomaticus* muscles of the face. This is the real Duchenne smile, authentic and heartfelt. Dr. Fredrickson says this puts people in a receptive mode, rather than being defensive, which they may be when they see a fake smile. Dr. Fredrickson relates it to children beaming and smiling and being ready to learn. They're telling you in a way, "Come teach me something," or "Come be with me!" This is an authentic innocent smile.

Some people think of a smile as a way to influence other people, a manipulative expression. But what we're talking about here is a smile that is totally disarming, a smile that shows that you are receptive and ready to learn from the other person. Such a smile is safe to share. Thus, in our research, we've found that an authentic smile indicates openness and willingness to learn new information, which could be a key to learning and successful negotiations.

On Dr. Fredrickson's website is a paper by Johnson and Fredrickson that goes into the research proving that "own-race bias" or "same-race bias" can be transcended with positive emotions and smiling.

Most people are only able to accurately understand subtle differences of facial expression and emotion in their own race. Positive emotions and smiling are the exception to the rule; they seem to transcend racial bias. People can see that a smile is a smile is a smile, no matter what racial group the smile is coming from.

Thus, smiling is an invitation to transcend racial and cultural barriers. The smile is an open invitation to not judge individuals by their culture, but be open to receiving this transcendentally positive emotional expression from them.

This suggests a unique approach in global human relationships and intercultural relationships.

Positive emotions and accompanying facial expressions such as smiling can open a new era of ambassadorship and diplomacy. They can bring about new negotiations where peace talks have stalled. They can signal a global willingness to learn, grow, and share.

We are reminded here of quotes such as "Smiling has no accent" and "Smiling is a universal language." A smile has the same meaning in every culture. That's what Dr. Fredrickson is talking about here.

But Dr. Fredrickson says, "This same race bias can be transcended so that a cultural or global feeling of goodwill can become more evident through this language of positive emotion and smiling." The authentic Duchenne smile is that "language of positive emotion and smiling." It is a true lie detector that demonstrates to others your openness to their belief systems and truths. The true honest smile of the heart, the honest smile spreading across the face with those crinkled corners beside the eyes, shows that the smile is heartfelt. It brings a glow.

The Duchenne smile can be seen as an indicator of openness to cultural and global peace—peace within oneself as well as peace between countries and nations. I'm determined to prove that smiling—smiling from the heart, smiling from within, smiling to show openness and a willingness to learn, smiling as a way of accepting, growing, and sharing—is the key to world peace and personal peace. Smiling is an invitation to dialogue—a healing dialogue, a peace negotiation dialogue. It shows a willingness to expand one's relationships.

I commented to Dr. Fredrickson that a non-authentic smile seems to reflect cynicism or even criticism. Dr. Fredrickson agreed, saying that there is research to show that a fake smile could be as destructive as, if not more so than, no smile at all. And this comes from biochemical and psychological research, no less.

Dr. Fredrickson cited two different studies showing that non-authentic smiles could provoke negative biochemistry. One study was by Richard Davidson, who looked at prefrontal left and right hemisphere activity in the brain. Smiling had a profound positive or negative effect, depending on whether the smile was sincere or not. Davidson has done extensive studies on monks who sat in long-term silent meditation, sometimes for days at a time. He has also been quoted widely regarding his research with the Dalai Lama.

I asked Dr. Fredrickson if there was one element that really stood out in her research to show the beneficial social effects of smiling. She said, "I think the most important thing is to have a better, healthier sense of social awareness. In other words, when people are smiling and have that type of positive emotion, they generally think in terms of 'we.' Thus they can negotiate around differences of opinion, but instead of thinking 'me and you' or 'me against you,' they're thinking, 'we,' and I think that is a very important thing to remember. It sort of implies what we have in common and not our differences, and that helps to unite us, rather than divide us—and I think smiling does this really well."

And I would say that it's more a sense of "we" working together rather than "me against you."

"If you wake up with a smile or a frown, then your day will be accordingly. Obviously so much of life is how we perceive it and if you perceive it with a smile, then you will probably be a lot happier. *Try smiling* and see why!"

—*Fred Hemmings*
Senator, Hawaii State Legislature
Worldwide surfing legend and pioneer

Smile Like a Star

by Bob Delmonteque

"There is much scientific as well as anecdotal research about the power of your smile. All of my world-famous clients were famous because of their endearing and charismatic smiles…the same smiles that you possess."
—Bob Delmonteque

I know the power of the human smile firsthand.

I have been a professional coach to actors, actresses, and models in Hollywood since the 1940s and have also coached many bodybuilders, business and corporate people, and politicians both young and old.

Some of my clients in Hollywood have included Marilyn Monroe, Betty Grable, Clark Gable, Errol Flynn, Douglas Fairbanks Jr., Rita Hayworth, Marlon Brando, Johnny Weissmuller, Buster Crabbe, Chuck Norris, Linda Grey, Tyrone Power, and lately actors like Matt Dillon—all of them famous for their smiles.

Marilyn Monroe was probably the most amazing of all of these, with her cheerful and attractive smile that most of us became familiar with during her career. All the big movie studios had gyms for their actors and actresses to work out in, and Marilyn was the least inclined to work out and exercise, yet she had the biggest and brightest smile of them all that I remember.

Errol Flynn liked to work out the most of all the celebrities I trained and coached in Hollywood. Not only was he extremely vivacious, but his smile could almost light up the room when he came in.

Clark Gable was one of my favorite students and also one of the most charismatic; a great part of his charisma came from his healthy, easy smile. A lot of women fell in love with his smile throughout his career.

Johnny Weissmuller, who played Tarzan, trained with weights tied on his legs when he was swimming, either in Hollywood or in Hawaii with Duke Kahanamoku. Johnny had the healthiest broad smile—the smile of a true athlete—and it was one of the strong successes of his personality and his career.

I trained Rock Hudson throughout his career, and his smile was undoubtedly stellar and a great part of his stardom. He was dynamic and authentic, and when he smiled it made friends and fans for a lifetime.

I trained and coached quite a few corporate executives like business tycoon H. L. Hunt and many of the top Texas Oil men. Even they had to use sincere smiles to build relationships in their demanding corporate lives and with others.

Whenever I talked with John F. Kennedy, he shared a warm and true smile with me, and that was one of the reasons that President Kennedy was the most endearing president of all time. He had the best smile I can think of, and he smiled frequently and warmly in a way that made me feel both comfortable and respected.

I trained the original astronauts in Houston for a long time, and Alan Shepard was most notable in the area of smiling. Heads turned when he walked by.

Another astronaut I trained who had a healthy, spontaneous smile was James Lovell, who went on to become a famous politician as well. James was known for his infectious and easygoing smile.

You can see the smiles of these astronauts if you look at any group photo with the other astronauts. It's interesting that they had the same charisma as the Hollywood stars, and their smiles were a great part of that.

Over many years of knowing and working with famous professional boxer Rocky Marciano, I had a chance to see that despite his reputation for being a tough and rough fighter, Rocky was actually an incredibly nice and considerate person who was warm and affectionate. And Rocky had one of the best smiles you could ask for.

I am 85 years old now, so I have seen hundreds of professional careers that depended upon excellent smiles—smiles that could entrance and empower as well as attract.

From my experience with celebrities and famous names, I can say with absolute certainty that a brilliant smile is the most important element in the success of an actor, actress, model, or even athlete!

The power of the human smile creates many neurological and biological pathways for increased energy and stamina, and it hardwires the brain and emotions to be in an optimum state.

You might say smiles have been indispensable to all the famous people I have worked with over six decades of coaching and training famous names, faces, and bodies. Anyone who has a giant career in motion pictures or on the stage has an obligation to develop their smile capacity as much as they develop their acting and modeling. I can hardly think of any person in this industry who has succeeded without a great smile that people can relate to.

The important thing to remember is that the smile can affect the physical body and your biochemistry. This fact is really important to those people who are literally on call all the time to be charismatic and energetic. A true honest smile is like an electric magnet—it can turn on your charisma and power and influence others in the most beneficial way. I have seen it demonstrated profoundly thousands of times with the top names I have trained and coached over the past 50 years.

Charisma and attractiveness are almost synonymous with smiling. Who could even begin to separate a strong smile and self-esteem? Self-esteem is usually accompanied by a smile of some type, and the human face is extremely talented in its ability to show a person's state of mind and body through a smile or the lack of a smile.

In Hollywood, when I coached professional actors and actresses, there was an obvious need for my famous clients to develop their personal smile capacity right along with their social skills, strength, fitness, and etiquette. Many of the top names I coached and taught were famous because of their memorable and well-photographed smiles. Their faces are still remembered to this day in the smiling images memorized by their fans.

Most people would consider my work in coaching and training to be limited to physical fitness training, but I must always be aware of and convey the total range of dynamic health and positive psychology to get my clients' physical health up to the optimum level.

Until now, this research did not exist in any substantial collection. What we have now is a complete and detailed overview of the astounding research on the importance of smiling for every aspect of happy living and top health.

Since I have been told many times that my own smile is attractive and healing in itself, I know that what we put on our faces can affect our relationships and our own health. More than a few times in my professional career in Hollywood, I honestly told my clients who acted and modeled that their smiles made me feel great. Their smiles made up a major percentage of their charisma and talent. What better way to keep their fans returning time and again to their films and productions?

People want to feel good, and they inherently know right away that a smile makes something in their hearts, minds, and bodies feel very good. The public is always ready and primed to receive a smile, and there is a good reason for this. A smile from a celebrity, a sports figure, a friend, or a loved one will bring a smile to your own face, and that automatically makes you feel on top of everything—in a "peak state," as Charles Garfield (author of *Peak Performance*) says.

One thing has not changed that much: people know that smiling empowers them and their careers and health, as does seeing a smile on another. If you randomly polled people around you and asked whether they preferred to see a smiling person or smile themselves, or to see a frowning person or frown themselves, they would generally choose the smile. The reason is obvious.

Wherever my students went, people wanted their smiles as much as or more than their autographs. They were always bringing sunshine to the sets and the film crews by smiling and laughing, and this always impressed me about their personalities.

Marilyn Monroe was such a great smile personality—always generous in sharing her joy and bringing smiles to all around her, as well as to her many fans around the world. She always gave me a smile when I saw her, which, needless to say, felt great.

A lot of the famous faces I trained in film industry circles were known for their smiles. The smiles were direct links to their energetic personalities, which drew people to their movies.

The other fact that is so important to realize is that the self-esteem of even the most common people is elevated when they smile or receive smiles from others. That is why cosmetic dentists make a fortune, especially in New

York and Hollywood. Smiles equal successful careers and even self-esteem!

The bottom line is that CEOs and celebrities of all types have to have great smiles. There is a link in people's minds between a smile and reliability and trust. The smile is an all-pervasive tool when it comes to relationships and social influence, and the smile is a tool for achieving total health and fitness as well as warm and caring relationships.

Take a tip from the famous and the wealthy: smile like a star!

★★★★★

About Bob Delmonteque:

Bob Delmonteque (Malibu, California), has been trainer and coach to thousands of Hollywood stars, CEOs, astronauts and athletes since 1940. His website: *www.bobdelmonteque.com*

"Much of our time is spent working so diligently at improving ourselves and our lot in life. I am among those in the thick of it, coaching others to do so as they discover their *ho'ohana*, their on-purpose intention and passion in the work they do, as a celebration of the *Aloha* spirit naturally innate in them.

"I often find that we make it so much harder than it has to be; however, now we have much new research on the importance of smiling and inspiration for more *aloha* with ease. Smiling is a way to share our *aloha* instantly, and so naturally we *must* smile more for our own well-being; in doing so, we share contagiousness of spirit, inspiring us so joyously. *Smile* and know the joy you were meant to feel in each living moment."

—*Rosa Say*
Founder and head coach,
Say Leadership Coaching
Author of *Managing with Aloha,*
Bringing Hawaii's Universal
Values to the Art of Business

Let a Smile Be Your Umbrella

© *Brian Luke Seaward*

I am sitting on my red flagstone patio looking at a beautiful Rocky Mountain sunset. There is a big grin on my face, but it's not solely because of the crimson and orange clouds floating over the alpine peaks. Piped into my ears through the wondrous technology of my Apple iPod and headphones is a soundtrack of music that makes me smile from ear to ear. It's feel-good music—a mix of songs that I compiled to lift my spirits from wherever they might happen to be and place them on Cloud Nine.

A song performed by a Hawaiian group called Hapa brings back memories of Maui, and once again the mountains meet the sea. The music's magic is definitely working because I am feeling euphoric, tapping my feet to the rhythm. With the view looking west and a soundtrack to match, I have surpassed Cloud Nine and am headed for a cloud in the high teens.

Simply *nirvana*. Music has a way of stirring the emotions, at least mine, and I am ever so grateful.

Truth be told, there are hundreds, perhaps thousands, of things that can bring a smile to my face. I marvel at the sprouting of blossoms on slumbering cherry trees each spring. I take delight in the sight of the first hummingbird at my feeder.

Perhaps most of all, I smile to my heart's content when I gaze up at the sky filled with stars, which elicits a whole new level of wonder and curiosity. The eyes may be the windows to the soul, but the smile is a window to the heart, and my heart runneth over with joy.

As a health psychologist—one who honors the integration, balance, and harmony of mind, body, spirit, and emotions—I have always been fascinated with positive emotions and their effects on the human condition.

Research in this field reveals that optimism tends to boost the integrity of the immune system. In 1990, while I was on the faculty of the American University in the nation's capital, I taught a popular course called "Humor and Health." Based on the premise of the new discipline of psychoneuroimmunology (*e.g.*, endorphins, neuropeptides, and mind-body-spirit healing), this course became a field study in smiles, giggles, and laughter through movies, jokes, music, and guest speakers, including Art Buchwald and Patch Adams, M.D.

It was the one class that I taught in a career spanning over three decades that no student ever skipped. In fact, many students brought their girlfriends, boyfriends, roommates, friends, and even parents to class. It became obvious from the first night that a smile is infectious and laughter is contagious.

One of the premises of the Humor and Health course was a statement from the patron saint of humor therapy, Norman Cousins, who said that each and every one of us must take responsibility for our own health and well-being. This responsibility includes emotional balance—in this case, making time for episodes of comic relief as a respite from the stress of everyday life.

Rather than have my students write a term paper, a common type of assignment in college courses, I took a more practical approach to teaching this course. I explained that the average child laughs about 300–400 times a day. Adults, on the other hand, have narrowed this number down to 15. Hospital patients (and this has actually been studied) laugh zero times per day.

Taking the lead from Norman Cousins, I invited each student to create a "tickler notebook." Each student was assigned to compile jokes, photos, birthday cards, JPG files, Dear Abby letters, Dave Barry columns, cartoons, and anything else that would bring a smile to their faces and warm their hearts.

The real purpose of the "tickler notebook" was to redirect their conscious attention to focus on the positive side of life every now and then. In doing so, it was my hope that they would establish a sense of emotional levity against a backdrop of mounting personal responsibility and ever-increasing social ills. I also advised that should they ever end up in the hospital, this humor Rx would only help augment their healing process.

Years later, it's not uncommon for me to receive occasional e-mails or cards from former students, telling me that they're on their fifth tickler notebook.

Smile!

Nowadays, whenever I speak on the topic of humor and healing, I give the same homework assignment to anybody within earshot (though I never collect the notebooks).

Whether we are college students, corporate executives, housewives, or nurses, we each need to take responsibility for our health, and comic relief is a great way to start. On more than one occasion, I have had strangers walk up to me, show me a tickler notebook, and politely ask for a grade. In the process, we both smile.

We live in a very stress-filled world today, a world filled with negativity and fear. The daily news is chock-full of items and stories that only perpetuate this negativity (by the way, consider *not* watching the news—you'll feel so much better).

Moreover, many people today have a passive (rather than active) existence, living vicariously through reality TV shows and tabloid magazines. Rather than letting technology serve us, we have become slaves to it, with a growing dependence that in some cases leads to addiction.

It doesn't have to be this way. Taking responsibility means seizing the day by finding something new to stimulate your mind and raise your spirits.

Taking responsibility is as simple as stepping outside and feeling the wind on your face and the sunshine on your arms. Bringing a smile to your face is as simple as finding something funny or comical…every day.

Several years ago, I took a trip to Ireland with my sister, Gail, to celebrate her 30th birthday. In an effort to reclaim our Irish heritage, we toured the Dingle Peninsula and Ring of Kerry, and we even saw all "40 shades of green." On the taxi ride from the airport in Shannon, our cabbie was all smiles. After we introduced ourselves and he learned of our Irish ancestry, he gave us a Reader's Digest version of Irish history all the way up to the potato famine of 1918.

"The Irish have not had it easy," he said, "but through it all, we have adapted." In an Irish brogue thick enough to cut with a knife, he said, "Do you know why I smile?" Before we could answer, he continued, "Well, let me tell you. A smile is one of life's simple pleasures, and it costs absolutely nothing. Add some great fiddle music and dancing and what could be better than that, I ask you?"

We just smiled at him and then at each other, because we knew he was right. His parting words to us were, "Let a smile be your umbrella, always."

What makes me smile? My answer might sound like a version of "My Favorite Things"—not the least of which is raindrops on roses. In truth, my list is nearly endless, perhaps because I keep adding to it each day. I never cease to be amazed at life, from the simple to the pro-found, from the ordinary to the extraordinary.

So here is a question for you: What makes you smile? What makes you giggle and laugh? Grab a pen and paper and start making a list. Keep a copy in your wallet or purse. Put copies on your fridge and bathroom mirror.

This will become your Smile Rx.

* * * * *

About Brian Luke Seaward, Ph.D.:
Brian Luke Seaward, Ph.D., is recognized internationally for his expertise on the topics of holistic stress manage-ment, mind-body-spirit healing, and human spirituality. He is the author of the acclaimed textbook, *Managing Stress,* and the bestselling books, *Stand Like Mountain, Flow Like Water; The Art of Calm, Quiet Mind; Fearless Heart;* and *Stressed Is Desserts Spelled Backward*. He can be reached at *www.brianlukeseaward.net*.

"The first act of diplomacy and world peace should be a *Smile*…you should give and receive as many *Smiles* as you can. I've learned that a *Smile* is the universal language uniting all people.

"One of the greatest gifts you can give as well as receive is a *Smile*. And to think it costs you nothing.

"Sometimes when our world is upside down, our smile is upside down. Time for a somersault or handstand or just *Smile!* Only bodybuilders should frown—since experts tell us it takes more effort and muscles to frown, they are just muscle-building. Everyone else will find it easier to *Smile*.

Just think—if my ancestors had started my name with S instead of ending it with s, my name would be Smile instead of Miles!"

—*Robert Miles*, author of
Warren Buffett Wealth

Celestial Smiling: Mo Siegel

by Elan Sun Star

"The human smile is the most amazing of our gifts as human beings. I travel all over the world and spend a lot of time in corporate board meetings and airports and traveling and I meet a lot of people. The smiling faces that I am blessed to see are one of my greatest gifts, especially that of my wonderful wife."
—*Mo Siegel* Founder of Celestial Seasonings, Board of Whole Foods

Talking about the idea of spreading a smile or a good feeling around the world with the least amount of effort and financing, I had an opportunity to interview my friend Mo Siegel, who started the company Celestial Seasonings in the early 1970s in Boulder, Colorado.

At the time, he was severely limited by funding, picking wild herbs in the mountains of Boulder, and sewing them up in cloth bags; but Mo had a dream of expanding Celestial Seasonings to the next level.

The delightfully illustrated boxes of Celestial Seasonings teas that are now piled high on multiple shelves in health food and grocery stores have possibly spread smiles to the faces of more people than any product in the world. The quotes, pictures, and artwork on the boxes

 of Celestial Seasonings teas, and the tea inside, have brought contentment and warmth to hundreds of millions of people on hundreds of millions of cold nights around the world. The comfort of the tea, the inspirational quotes on the boxes, and the beautiful artwork have certainly served to bring smiles to many people.

Mo Siegel is now one of the directors of Whole Foods Market, another global business endeavoring to bring consciousness and health to people's dinner plates in the same way that Celestial Seasonings brought consciousness and relaxation to people's teacups.

If you aren't familiar with Celestial Seasonings teas, they are blends of herbal teas that were originally developed for the health food market; but they have since spread to grocery stores on a much wider level and become a global product. Celestial Seasonings was listed on the *New York Times* and *Wall Street Journal*'s list of 100 businesses that any corporate CEO would want to head, because Celestial Seasonings was a global success financially and a win-win cooperative venture with quite happy employees.

When I asked Mo about smiling while he flew around the world dealing with Whole Foods corporate business, he replied as follows:

"Let me give you an example out of my own home life. I have a friend who's a very accomplished man, who's extremely creative and active around the world in his business and his home life. He's stayed at my house before and he tends to meditate in long periods or do contemplative prayer work, and my children have told me that when he's sitting in meditation for a long period of time, he has this goofy smile on his face. And my children have told me the same thing—that when I am in extended periods of peaceful meditation, that I have the same goofy smile on my face. And when I look at my friend and his so-called goofy smile, I realize there's something going on in his soul. It's not a frown, not at all—it's a smile! And it shows up on his face.

"And of course, your smile radiates from who you are inside your soul. You can't really fake a smile. It's your calling card. And if you're happy inside, it does show on your face. So a smile is a really good indicator for me.

"But of course, even if you do have to learn to smile, by just practicing it every day, we earn those wrinkles from the smile on the eyes in the face, and those are good wrinkles, those lines on the face. Those wrinkles are a sign of optimism, happiness, and joy and goodwill. Those smile lines on your face are a sign of growth, as far as I'm concerned. I couldn't run a big business without them. And Mark Twain said, 'Wrinkles around the eyes and mouth are just signs where smiles have been.'

"The wrinkles around your eyes from smiling all the time say a lot about who you are. And they're not just from weathering of the skin or old age; they're actually from smiling all the time. Of course, you always feel more comfortable around people who do.

"And of course, it's obvious to anybody that smiling makes you feel better. It makes you feel much better than frowning, and it makes other people feel better.

And it certainly opens the door. You can't have a great relationship without a smile upon your face. For example, nothing in my world is as beautiful as the smiles on the faces of my wife and my family.

"Out of everything in nature and this creation, the smile on the face of my wife means more to me than anything, and it represents all good things. I don't see how I could have been part of running a large corporation that ended up being a global success unless I had smiling as an asset on my side—both smiling employees and my own smile—to remind us all that we really were on each other's team."

Mo Siegel is quite well known, almost like a celebrity, because Celestial Seasonings teas have become part of the lives of so many people, including spiritual leaders, health foodies, meditation practitioners, and athletes. Celestial Seasonings is one of the most conscious beverage companies in the world, and Mo is an incredible businessman, but he's also a spiritual leader of sorts. His insights delving into creation and the Creator spread out into his daily life and his relationships with his team, staff, employees, and family.

He has a great philosophy of how to make his spiritual beliefs work in business and the practical world of daily life. Thus, his insights about the value of smiling in his family life and in his business and team life are a great example that it's more than just feeling good—it's a matter of a smile carrying you to the next level, where you can integrate the good feeling into your relationships with everyone around you, be it in business, home life, or friendships. A smile can do it all.

Mo continued, "I do know when I go into a business deal or a corporate meeting, or even a new friendship, that when I see the other person smiling, there's an open door to a great relationship, a new relationship, a business solution. And I consider smiling a great indicator to break the ice if there's any hesitation about a business deal or a new friendship. If a smile is so valuable on one level, why can't it be in business, too?"

Mo Siegel, already a global success on every level, says, "It's a sign of goodwill. A smile is an invitation to open up and talk, to dialogue, to share, to see what we have in common. I would even go so far as to say a smile is hope."

And I agree with Mo that a smile is one of the greatest indicators of goodwill in business relationships, global negotiations, peace negotiations, national and cultural interventions, or any situation where goodwill can help improve communications.

A smile is more than just feeling good. Separating that from our daily life, we must learn that smiles are our greatest asset, our greatest currency for creating goodwill and for improving communications, physical health, and mental and emotional well-being. It works in business; it works in international communications. Smiling should be part of the *modus operandi* of the United

Nations, even. I'm serious.

The Kindling Smile: Dee Coulter

by Elan Sun Star

I spoke to another creative teacher, lecturer, and writer, Dee Coulter, Ed.D., director of Kindling Touch Institute and a nationally recognized neuroscience educator. Her main interests have been learning patterns, music education, and teaching learners how to work with their brains to optimize learning. Dee was quite familiar with some of the work on facial expressions and smiling.

The work of Steven Porges, Robert Zajonc, and others sheds light on the role of smiling. Smiling seems to be the first method of actual survival and taking care of yourself. It's absolutely essential, and that's why it's there at birth, especially in the bonding with the mother. It may even be a way to disarm any potential harm.

Thus, I think we see that the term "a disarming smile" actually has a literal meaning. A "disarming smile" disarms others of any potential harmful intentions.

For a baby, it's an instinctual activity. It's almost a first introduction into the world. It's an instinctive endeavor to bond with the caregiver and create a good relationship. That's why babies smile, or at least that's what this research seems to show.

Since babies can't use the "fight or flight" response, if they don't bond with their caregivers and especially with their mothers by smiling, they drop into a "learned helplessness" and there is little they can do besides withdrawing. This withdrawal can shut down the baby's growth process and weaken the immune system. In severe cases where babies are neglected, a prolonged lack of attention can even be fatal. Creating a bond with a caregiver is what all mammals do. They have a long period of bonding with a caregiving parent, and a smile is the best way of creating a caring, trusting relationship right upon birth.

Dee says, "You can assume that if nature employs smiling and bonding at birth, it suggests that smiling is the most optimal way of creating this bonding. It's almost a basic suggestion, then, that because it is instinctive at the beginning and the baby smiles without any prompting, usually, these instincts or reflexes are nature's way of saying, 'You might want to try this. We've found it to be useful for your species.'"

Indeed, our species of humans has found it quite successful to smile all the way from birth to death. That smiling creates relationships, both with the outer world and our inner sense of peace and goodness.

In fact, Dee says, "It is nature's way of rekindling the 'best foot forward.'" And she says, "Since it's happening at such an unbelievably young age, even *in utero* or at birth, smiling definitely is preprogrammed in to be a healthy response.

"So in that first incident, almost like a whisper from the universe, from evolution—it just has a hint of the evolutionary trait that babies that smile and bond with their parents are happier and healthier, and there's more relationships, and, of course, that's an evolutionary plus. And then as the baby grows up, it finds that it can actually consciously do this, and it will revert to it, because it worked at birth and it worked as an evolutionary trait from the species.

"Now the baby can choose to use smiling in its relationship with the world and with itself. So when the baby learns to do things intentionally, and not just automatically, it can resort to the smile consciously, and choose to smile, which it generally does in society. Smiling is very normal.

"So it's almost as if we can be born with an automatic response or reflex, which is actually preprogrammed into the consciousness of the species and evolution. But it's with conscious intention that we make the choice to smile, that we come to another level of choosing the empowerment that smiling can bestow upon us."

Dee continues, "For some strange reason, researchers continue to ask the question, 'Well, how do babies learn to smile when they haven't been taught?' But they're not learning, it's already preprogrammed into their evolutionary hard drive. They already know to smile, because evolution says, 'Do this, it'll help you.' They don't seem to realize that it's not learned, it's automatic."

But if you keep smiling automatically, it doesn't have the power of an intentional smile. There is a sort of empowerment in knowing that you can smile that smile. There is an art to smiling an authentic smile that brings a beneficial result—either from a caregiver, in the case of a child, or in adult relationships, including your inner relationships.

Unfortunately, though, when the child is growing up, reinforcement is needed. Even for a small baby, if something as beautiful as a smile is not rewarded, it may be forgotten and its bounty lost. In other words, if we don't reward people who smile at us with a smile in return, they may forget the simple joy of a smile. What does this mean?

When people give us a gift by smiling at us, we should return the smile, or offer another gift as beneficial as their smile. If we don't reward the activity, the activity isn't reinforced. Sometimes you have to reinforce basic good traits, and smiling is a very good trait.

That's why smiling is already instinctively programmed into us by many generations of human beings. If people keep the habit of smiling, but there's no intention or heart in it—in other words, if they only see fake smiles— they will see what looks like a smile, but if the eyes aren't involved, if there's no heart in it, there's just a smile.

At least half of the smile is there in the eyes—the authentic Duchenne crinkle at the corners of the eyes, the windows to the soul.

Dee Coulter went on to talk about smiles as blessings. During her years on the faculty of Naropa University in

Boulder, Colorado, she developed a deep appreciation for the work of Vietnamese Buddhist monk Thich Nhat Hanh, renowned for his work with meditation, forgiveness, love, and the healing aspects of those modalities. Dee referred to his book, *Being Peace,* when she said, "You see, some people use a smile as a blessing, and Thich Nhat Hanh uses a smile as a blessing rather than just projecting his personality."

Take those words to heart. We can bless our external environment and ourselves by radiating warmth and goodwill to the world through a smile.

There are different qualities of smiling. Smiling as a form of blessing is one of the most important. It can be used to bless ourselves, others, and everything around us, even objects and living things that are not human. Smile at plants, smile at yourself in the mirror, smile at animals, smile at nature—smile at all of creation, nothing less. A smile is a blessing, and to bless and be blessed in return could be the most important aspect of smiling.

Another metaphor about smiling is that it's almost like hugging at a distance. You can allow people to maintain their privacy and their sense of personal space by smiling instead of hugging. Some people may feel threatened by a hug. You don't need to threaten them by touching them or moving into their personal space—you can hug at a distance with a smile.

There's a real benefit—a form of unconditional love—to allowing other people their own space, and at the same time, smiling at them as a blessing and an acknowledgment.

You can show your delight in another person with a quiet smile of benevolence. Whether the person is a child or an adult, you don't need to interfere unduly in his or her world. You don't need to demand an acknowl-edgment or offer a hug to show your delight. You don't need to draw the person into conversation. A simple smile gives the person room to receive the smile if they are so inclined and to learn from the world at their own pace, and allows you to express your appreciation at a distance.

Kindling Touch Institute's website is at www.kindlingtouch.com.

☼

"It is good to note that smiling has good physiological effects."

—*Anson Chong,*

Senator from Hawaii

Believe in Your Smile: Bruce Lipton, Ph.D.

by Elan Sun Star

"Smiling can transform your cellular
metabolism and your effect on the face of
every human being you encounter daily.
Through the effect of "mirror" neurons your
smile will spread automatically, producing
more infectious smiles, and then real global
transformation will happen."
—*Bruce Lipton, Ph.D.*

Dr. Bruce Lipton is a research
scientist, cell biologist, and
global speaker on the subject
of cellular metabolism, cell
consciousness, and beliefs;
he is also the author of *The
Biology of Belief*. Dr. Lipton
obtained his Ph.D. from the
University of Virginia, then
taught histology, cell biology, and embryology at
the University of Wisconsin
School of Medicine. Lipton went on to study quantum
physics and was also a research scientist at the Stanford
University School of Medicine. Lipton's published papers
on epigenetics pioneered the work proving that envi-

ronment and nurture affect the genes and alter their structure.

Dr. Lipton first became interested in cell biology when he saw live cells under a microscope in the second grade. In the undergraduate program at the University of Virginia, his studies included cellular biology and electron micros-copy. He also did pioneering work in stem cell research in 1967, long before the news headlines of the past few years.

One of the most important aspects of smiling is the bio-chemistry it creates and the change in the actual genetic structure of our cells. As far back as 30 years ago, Dr. Lipton discovered that the environment cells lived in affected their genetic structure. And because part of that environment includes emotions and the muscle structure of the face, his work is all about smiling. He found that the environment and nurturing affected the inherited characteristics of cells as much as genetic structure, although DNA is traditionally thought to play such a vital role. Lipton sees the cell's genetic structure as being little more than the reproductive core of cell biol-ogy. That is the key focus of epigenetics.

Dr. Lipton's insights into the value of smiling are quite unique, considering his pioneering background and his personal clarity and insights regarding other factors that change our RNA and DNA structures. Lipton's work is with the *brain* of the cell, which is what we're talking about altering when we alter consciousness by smiling and by working the muscles of our face.

Altering consciousness through smiling, dramatically affects every one of the 50 trillion cells in the body.

Studying cell "brains" (RNA, DNA, and mitochondria) helped Lipton realize that the brain of the cell acts and operates in much the same way as the human brain. By studying one, you can realize the results in another.

A cell's expression and health is a reflection of its environment—not just the biochemical environment, but also the emotional and physical. If we maintain an outlook that is positive, supportive, loving, and nurturing, our cells will adjust their biology to survive (and yes, to thrive) in that environment.

In a supportive environment full of smiles, the positive effect is measurably more beneficial than in an environment filled with negativity from frowning and arguing.

Indeed, smiling is a key factor here. Dr. Lipton says, "Both the human, the total human of 50 trillion cells, and each one of the 50 trillion cells adjust its biology and its consciousness to environmental stimuli good or bad, and will change its genetics and its biochemistry as the whole of

50 trillion cells and also every cell will adjust, and therefore a smile has a dramatic effect upon the belief system of the cell and the whole body."

Dr. Lipton says the *perception* of a smile—receiving a smile—is a very important environmental signal that stimulates the physiology through what are called "mirror neurons." Through these mirror neurons, we automatically mimic activities we see outside of ourselves. We can mimic the activity of anything in our environment.

When someone smiles at you and you smile back, that is a form of mirroring, or immediate positive feedback. Mirroring neurons are very, very important to understand. Don't underestimate the value of these neurons in helping you evolve.

Neurolinguistic programming practitioners (NLP) claim that we can mirror activities, copying any physical action that we have seen others perform. It sounds simplistic, but it is true that we can learn new activities quickly and easily. Mirror neurons show us how; they allow us to do something as simple as responding to a smile with a smile.

That's what we do in life. That's why we smile at others in response to their smiles. That is how the beneficial smiling virus spreads. You smile at others, they see that it makes you feel good, and they respond in kind. It's a win-win situation. If we spread the beneficence of this euphoric smile around the world, soon everyone will interpret life as positive rather than negative, constructive rather than destructive.

A smile from the mother at birth gives the child a behavior that the mirror neurons can reflect back. Thus, the smile is a universal language that starts at birth. The smiling face of the parent helps the baby feel a rush of endorphins for the first time, and the baby is thus assured that the environment is safe for them. The opposite is true as well: a look of concern, doubt, or fear on the face of a parent will be mirrored by the baby, who may well learn to pull away from intimate contact rather than gladly embrace the love that can be conveyed by a smile. The smile is a simple way to feel good.

And of course, a smile equals YES! That's wonderful. That actually gives a newborn baby a lot of information, just from a simple smile. Very early in life, as early as birth, we begin to connect feeling good and feeling safe with the smile that we learn from our parents. A smile indicates safety and the goodwill of the caretakers, the parents.

Dr. Lipton explains the science behind this. When we smile, we generate a neural pathway in the brain. That neural pathway soon sees another smile being mirrored back at it from a friend, a parent, or a new acquaintance; the mirror neurons are stimulated and they follow the same neural pathway, allowing an easy smile in return.

That's why it's so easy to get that good feeling. A smile is reciprocated immediately on the face of the person you smile at. It's almost automatic, and it's a healthy response. I smile at you, and you smile at me. See what a universal language this is? Thus, when you smile at me, it gives me the same physiological benefit as if I were initiating the smile myself.

The smiling virus spreads around the world and heals everyone. Dr. Lipton even says, "In truth, a smile would be contagious, like a virus. If I observe a smile in another, it will bring about a response in me, another smile. And thus it spreads down the line, the mirror neurons that are activated in me from seeing a smile will activate mine, and then my smile will activate the mirror neurons in another and so on and so on. You see the power of a smile to spread around the world, quickly, and a most wonderful and magical way. What else could equal a smile?"

Dr. Lipton continues, "Of course, if you smile, and it is contagious, which it is because of the biology behind it, then smiling really is a necessary exercise in life—essential, actually. Almost like a self-medication for you and those around you. And if you can feed that back into the system by noticing that you feel better when you smile, on all levels, for many reasons, and those around you feel better and want to repeat the smile because it is a feel-good medication, then it becomes a self-reinforced habit. By feeling good, you smile more, and by smiling more, you feel better; and by feeling better, you feel good, and everybody says, 'I want that, too.' And so they smile back automatically through their mirror neurons. Thus, smiling creates a self-generating cascade, an exponential expansion of good feeling around the world.

"I can actually tell the happiness ratio of the person and their psychology just from the condition of the cells. If there was a bad cellular metabolism, I could tell what the person or myself had been through, just by what shape the cells were in. Thus, bad cells and illness equals a negative attitude and a lack of smiling. Thus, if the cells didn't look good, you could say, 'Oh my goodness, there's something wrong here.'

"Smiling is a demeanor that you can actually express with your facial muscles. Smiling by its very nature implies that harmony is running through the system," Dr. Lipton says. "Smiling is one of the things that can increase exponentially the potential of jumping to a new level, socially and in biology, and actually reaching a threshold where we go to a whole new level of biochemistry and health.

"This is called 'spiking.' It reaches a threshold, and then everything 'spikes,' almost like a quantum leap. They spike into the next phase of growth and learning and optimum health. You literally 'jump' from one level to the next. Smiling can facilitate that dramatically. If only a relatively small amount of people were smiling consistently, it would help us to get to that threshold transformation of society and, of course, our own 50 trillion cells in our body, which is a society."

A small percentage of people smiling in the world can change the course of history, moving it away from war and destruction toward personal satisfaction and growth of the arts, the sciences, and health. So smiling can even be a uniting factor. Incoherence has proven to be destructive to metabolism; as the metabolism becomes more coherent and more orderly, there is more health and more happiness.

Consciousness is your ability to have the feedback—to see how you're fitting into the world, and how you're acting and feeling, and the effect that has upon both the world and your internal biochemistry, those 50 trillion cells you're composed of. A smile gives your body and mind a signal that you're satisfied with yourself and your life. It's a feedback loop that says, "Keep smiling, you're on the right track."

Dr. Lipton goes on to say, "This community of 50 trillion cells in your adult body has to learn how to become coherent, and smiling helps do that. And the cells in the body, once they cohere by realizing they can thrive rather than just survive—they can go beyond survival in the 50 trillion cells if they are synergistically cooperating. What a great role model for the 6 billion people on planet Earth to learn to cooperate synergistically, especially with something as simple as smiling. It doesn't take a big group effort, nor does it take a big budget. In fact, it takes no energy, and it gives you energy, and it costs nothing: it's free.

"If you can get 50 trillion citizens to live in harmony and coherence like you do when you smile to your 50 trillion cells, it helps us to get to that point socially where maybe 6 billion people, a minimal number, can work together in harmony and coherence toward a better society, the same way as it occurs in the body biochemically with the 50 trillion cells when you smile. This is all a very natural drive, and that's why it made you feel good to tell you it's good for everything. So if your 50 trillion cells feel good when you smile, then it signals the person around you who sees you smile; they pick up on all that energy, on how good it makes you feel. They know you are not faking it. And evolution says if it feels bad, don't do it again."

Dr. Lipton concludes, "When I first started to realize that I wasn't a victim and had a creative capacity in my own life, one of the problems was I started smiling so much it hurt, because I was smiling all the time, because I realized I really was creatively in control. And using the smile to control your filter of how you look at the world is one very important reason to smile for health, happiness and relationships. And once I realized the benefit of smiling, it became an eternal feature upon my face."

You can visit Dr. Lipton's websites at
www.liptonbiologyofbelief.com

www.brucelipton.com.

☼

Stress Management

by Jeff Gero, Ph.D.

Because I have deep interest and extensive knowledge in alternative health and healing modalities, people seek my advice and guidance to reduce stress and live happier lives. Learning the tremendous benefits of smiling is a must for anyone interested in their own health.

When I teach stress management programs to corporations and their executives, I tell participants to look in the mirror and have a good smile and allow that to grow into a laugh. This automatically sends a speedy message to the brain that everything is ok, which produces endorphins and other positive hormones while offsetting the negative effects of daily stress.

Smiling is not created by some occurrence or as the result of great and joyous conditions. Great and joyous conditions are created as the results of smiling. Belief precedes and produces experience. Smiling is a state of mind which will make you happy. Don't wait to smile—do it right now.

* * * * *

Jeff Gero is Program Director of *The Center for Wellbeing*; creator of the *Success Over Stress* Program; and author of *Secrets to Success at Work.*

☼

Smiling and Qi

by Katherine Orr

"Smile daily and you will become positively infected with uplifted spirit and a fresh infusion of joy!"
—*Kathy Orr* and *Master Qing Chuan Wang*

The greatest gifts are those that uplift the heart, nourish love, heal the spirit, and inspire joy. Smiling does this for us all.

We are reminded of the many healing benefits of a genuine smile. We learn about the effects of a smile on our physiology, read the words of scientists and poets, and are drawn toward the vision of a smiling, peaceful world.

Smiling is an uplifting experience. If you got out of bed on the wrong side this morning, try smiling and see what happens.

I speak from experience. My Chinese husband, a Qi Gong master from Shanghai, affirmed with a grin, "Smile, be happy—this is Tonic Number One!"

My husband is a sort of "smile master" in his own right. Through his Daoist (Taoist) tradition he is well acquainted with the heartfelt smile's relationship to health and self-healing, and he uses it every day in his Qi Gong. He trains his students to smile during Qi Gong practice (*relax*, *open*, *smile* are his three main directives), and a meditative smile plays on his lips as he performs "*qi* balancing" on clients during healing sessions.

What is a smile's relationship to health from the traditional Chinese perspective?

Ancient Chinese philosophy and traditional Chinese medicine, of which Qi Gong is a part, are based on the recognition of a subtle life-force energy that permeates and circulates through all things.

The Chinese call this energy *qi*.

When *qi* flows freely and smoothly through the body, it promotes health and well-being. When *qi* flow becomes blocked and unbalanced for long enough, physical diease follows.

What factors influence the quality and flow of the body's *qi*? Things such as the food we eat, the schedules we keep, and especially our attitudes, thoughts, and emotions.

A negative attitude and feelings of fear, anxiety, anger, sadness, hurt, and stress can cause our *qi* flow to contract, diminish, and become blocked and unbalanced.

A positive attitude and feelings of happiness, peace, joy, gratitude, appreciation, acceptance, trust, and contentment cause us to relax into our natural state, where *qi* can flow unimpeded in a balanced way.

All aspects of traditional Chinese medicine, including acupuncture, herbs, and Qi Gong, work toward a single goal: to restore the body's *qi* to a smooth, balanced flow.

Although we cannot control all aspects of life, we can control certain things, such as our diets, our schedules, and our attitudes. When we choose to open our hearts and *smile*, the good *qi* we generate promotes healing and happiness.

* * * * *

About Katherine Orr and Master Wang:

Katherine Orr is the author of *Beautiful Heart, Beautiful Spirit*, Shing-ling-mei Wudang Qigong as taught by Master Qing Chuan Wang. Her husband, Master Wang, is a Qi Gong grandmaster and holder of ancient lineage of Taoist Shing-ling-mei Wudang Qigong, licensed by the Chinese government.

Visit their website, *www.wudangqigong.com*.

"There are two kinds of people: Those who believe their lives are determined by forces outside themselves, and those who believe that their lives are determined by a Force inside themselves."

—*Alan Cohen*

"Smiling is our greatest asset: This simple skill (smiling) can change your life as well as the lives of others who come into your visual range. I often write on the power of smiling in my books and speak about it to corporate audiences globally in my lectures and keynotes speeches. It is one of the greatest human and corporate assets. Smile at someone today."

—*Tim Sanders*
Author of *The Likeability Factor: How to Boost Your L-Factor and Achieve Your Life's Dreams* and *Love Is the Killer App. New York Times* and international bestseller.
www.timsanders.com

"A smile carries many messages in its upturned mouth. It warms us with its 'yes.' Smiling instills us with its message of acceptance. Smiling inspires us with its amusement, giving us a magic passport into the world of Thalia, the Muse and guiding spirit of inspiration, creativity and comedy. She wears a smiling mask and invites us to join her. What better place to visit?

"At the Queen's Hospital in Honolulu, the staff all co-operates to create an atmosphere where smiles can transform health and lives."

—*Hob Osterlund*, RN, MS
Health, Humor and Hospitals,
Queen's Hospital, Honolulu, Hawaii
Producer, *www.chucklechannel.com*

The Smiling Breath

Copyright 2006 Dennis Lewis

"Smiling is science both ancient and modern. The power of a genuine smile to uplift our spirits and help heal us is profound and healing and empowering. Whether it is directed toward others or ourselves or is simply an expression of our innermost being, a genuine smile says 'yes' to the miracle and mystery of love and life."
—*Dennis Lewis*, author of *The Tao of Natural Breathing*

As I wrote in my book, *Free Your Breath, Free Your Life*, a genuine smile has the power not only to relax and benefit others, but also to bring about deep levels of relaxation in the one who is smiling. This is especially true in today's high-pressured world, where tense, frowning faces are the norm.

"The *smiling breath* practice that I offer below is for me a fundamental practice of both self-awareness and self-healing. The sensitive, relaxing energy field that it produces helps me observe by contrast the unhealthy tensions, attitudes, and habits that undermine my health and vitality." (From *The Tao of Natural Breathing*, Rodmell Press, 2006.)

I hope you will try this *smiling breath* practice often in your life. At times you may find it difficult to put a smile on your face and just keep breathing. There is a tendency in all of us, especially when we are anxious, stressed, or out of harmony with the present moment, to frown, hold our breath, or breathe very rapidly.

The last thing we are often willing to give up is our tension, unhappiness, and suffering. But if you can remember to try the simple practice below, you will soon learn how to open yourself to the transformative power of the *inner smile*—the transformative power of your own true identity.

* * * * *

Smiling Breath Practice

Wherever you are and whatever you are doing, begin this smiling breath practice by being present to how you are feeling physically, mentally, and emotionally, as well as how you are breathing.

Do you feel relaxed and happy, or do you feel tense and anxious?

What kinds of thoughts are you having?

Are you able to say "yes" to the present moment, or is the present moment your enemy?

Is your breathing open and comfortable, or is it tight and constricted?

Don't try to change anything. Simply be present, as best you can, to how you feel and what is happening within you. The beginning of real change is presence, the awareness of "what is."

Next, while breathing only through your nose, rub your hands together until they are very warm.

Put them on your belly.

Sense the warmth and energy coming from your hands, and watch how this sensation influences your breathing for at least two minutes.

As your belly naturally relaxes, you may notice that it begins to expand more on inhalation and retract more on exhalation. Let this process happen naturally. There should be no effort to push your belly out on the in-breath or pull it in on the out-breath.

Let your awareness of the warmth and sensation coming from your hands on your belly do all the work.

Now, with one hand on your heart and the other on your belly, smile to yourself. That's right: *put a smile on your face (and keep smiling)* even if you don't feel like it. Though your smile may seem totally artificial at the beginning, if you *keep smiling,* a transformation will soon take place.

As you continue smiling, notice how you begin to feel and appreciate the miracle of being alive—here and now.

Notice that the smile you are now experiencing is somehow part of your deepest essence. It is a manifestation of who you really are!

Now sense your in-breath entering through the smile on your face; have the sensation that you are inhaling "the breath of life," which itself is smiling, through your nose and face and all the way down into your heart and belly. On the out-breath, exhale slowly and gently through pursed lips, as though you were making a candle flame flicker (but not go out). Allow any tension or anxiety you may be experiencing to be released with the out-breath. And smile!

Then simply wait for the next inhalation to take place by itself, when it is ready. Allow yourself to be breathed by the moment itself.

Continue smiling and breathing in this way for several breaths. Your breath should remain very quiet, even inaudible.

Try this entire *smiling breath* practice whenever you can remember to do so, whenever you feel yourself becoming stressed out or anxious, or whenever you feel out of touch with who you really are.

If the circumstances you are in make it impossible to put your hands on your belly and heart, simply sense these areas with your inner attention as you smile and breathe.

The key is to keep a smile on your face and to breathe through the *smile*. When you are ready to stop, take an impression of how you feel, of your physical, mental, and emotional state, as well as how you are breathing. Notice any changes that have taken place.

Notice how this simple *smiling breath* practice has brought you a deep sense of inner stillness, calm, and happiness, and how it has brought you back into the miracle of the present moment.

And smile!

* * * * *

About Dennis Lewis:

Dennis Lewis, a longtime student of Taoism, Advaita, and the Gurdjieff Work, teaches natural breathing, Qi Gong, and self-inquiry. He is the author of *The Tao of Natural Breathing*, the three-CD audio program "Natural Breathing" (formerly titled "Breathing as a Metaphor for Living"), and *Free Your Breath, Free Your Life*. You can learn more about him and his work at *www.dennislewis.org*.

"Energetically an authentic smile brightens the aura or subtle energy body and promotes heart-to-heart connection. In my work with Barbara Brennan's techniques and direct perception of the human radiant aura, I can see and palpate this energy. It is bright and colorful in healthy people with good attitudes, and low and dull in people with distorted health and perceptions.

"All healing systems say simply 'good medicine' exists in a smile. In this world currently so impacted with negativity, war, hunger, disease, disaster, may we commit to the daily practice of smiling as a universal measure of love, peace, and joy. A smile is a harmless yet very powerful and healing measure which energetically and spiritually raises the planetary vibrational levels and promotes world peace."

—*Dr. Ruey Jane Ryburn*
Healer and professor emeritus,
University of Hawaii
School of Nursing
Graduate founder of *Sacred Path Healing* in Honolulu, Hawaii

The Healing Smile

by Cay Randall May

"In the medical research and in my intuitive
practice, there is a wealth of fantastic facts
on the power of smiling to transform our
physical, mental and emotional health as
well as our relations."
—*Cay Randall May*

As a practicing medical intuitive, I work in coordina-
tion with doctors and other healers by first bringing
to awareness the possible underlying causes of disease
and pain. In my work with Dr. Norm Shealy, M.D., and
others throughout the years pinpointing the specific
causes of ill health, I have found that whatever form it
takes, healing is not only structural and biochemical in
nature, but also a matter of attitude and outlook.

In our daily lives, we either practice a consistent healing
attitude or a non-healing attitude, and this perspective
on one's condition can make the difference between a
recovery of optimum health and a chronic problem.

Smiling is a personal choice to look at life and the healing process in a positive and therefore constructive manner, which is tremendously supportive to the process of
transforming disease into ease and thus into health. Since
smiling and interpreting our lives in a positive modality
produces an optimal state of psychology and biochemistry, it can be said to be an important element in keeping

the individual in the best place possible to avoid imbalances in the personality and body.

The causes of disease are manifold, and only trained physicians and doctors can diagnose the true cause of any disorder in the human mind and body.

We do know that an attitude of joy and optimism is essential, coupled with dealing with the disease on the basic level of nutrition, exercise, and surgery when necessary.

Even in this day of complementary medicine, a single type of healing will never take the place of a total approach, and at times physical measures are the most important medical response to a disorder.

Now, modern research has enough data to show that something as simple as smiling can indeed have a dramatic effect on the healing response as well as the desire to get well.

In his psychoneuroimmunology and endocrinology work at UCLA decades ago, Dr. Norman Cousins found that the patient's mind, emotions, and interpretation of a diagnosis all had a powerful effect on the outcome of healing.

Fear and negative emotions created a very poor terrain for healing to take place. Thus, a new science of emotional intelligence based on emotions and states of being in mind, body, and spirit has been integrated into modern medicine to the extent that it cannot be ignored in any healing procedure.

Smiling creates a host of beneficial results in a patient's hormones and physiological health, as well as a state of mental and emotional well-being; all of these are part of a balanced response to disease, in addition to the conventional medical interventions that are often unavoidable. As a trained and practicing medical intuitive, I help clients pinpoint specific possible causes of their ailments and then have their physicians check these possible causes. This quite often happens when an ailment cannot be accurately diagnosed or dealt with.

I feel that smiling, in its ability to transform attitude and change the interpretation of a situation from gloomy to positive and optimistic, can be a tremendous aid to the recovery of total health on all levels.

Without making any medical statements in relation to smiling and its ability to help the healing process, I can say it is obvious that my clients who choose to smile and carry a positive attitude heal faster and recover more fully than those who reside in a mental, emotional, and thus physical state of fear, doubt, and frowning.

Smiling can only help the overall healing process, and for this reason it should be included in one's daily routine of beneficial practices that support health and healing. I suggest that anyone wanting to maintain perfect health or to heal a serious disorder include smiling as a daily practice. It can only help.

* * * * *

Cay Randall May is a Medical Intuitive and the author of *Pray Together Now.*

"Heart disease is largely preventable with daily activity, a healthy diet and a positive outlook on life and actions like *smiling.* Although the latter is all too often underemphasized, recent studies suggest that positive emotions may indeed benefit the heart and smiling increases positive emotions in many ways.

"Thus, while we continue to explore the intricate relationship between the mind and cardiovascular system, *smiling* puts forth an outstanding and powerful testimonial for optimism, hope and connecting with others. Needless to say, *smiling* will do wonders for your heart and overall sense of well-being."

—Michael Miller, M.D.
Director, Center for Preventive Cardiology
University of Maryland Hospital,
Baltimore, Maryland

Listening to Smiles

by Kay Lindahl

How do you listen to a smile? How does smiling impact the way you listen? These two questions are not commonly asked, and yet listening is a key part of the outcome of smiles. Listening is also another facet of the pathway to peace. We must learn how to listen to each other in order to live together in peace. The combination of smiling and listening can lead us to new ways of being together, for a better world for all of us.

So, how do we listen to a smile? Listening involves all of our senses—not just our ears. When we are truly listening to other people, we are so totally present in the moment that we may not be aware of anything else. However, there are many factors that we are taking in at the same time. We hear their words, but we are also aware of their body language—the expressions on their faces, the looks in their eyes, the way they hold their bodies, other movements they are making—and the immediate surroundings, including such things as the temperature, the furnishings in the room, or other noises. Then there are those internal distractions—our own emotions, thoughts, and ideas that come up during this time. So there's a lot going on!

What happens when we see someone smile in a conversation? It usually makes us relax a bit, reduces any anxiety we might have had, and makes us feel more connected. Once we feel that the smile is authentic—often by seeing the eyes smile, too—then we lower our barriers and begin to let the other person in. We begin to see ourselves in relationship with the other person. We can notice our commonalities. There's more openness.

I'm reminded of a recent experience on a trip to Turkey. I was in a group of 12 Americans on an interfaith tour. We were walking in one of the large parks in Istanbul and came across a group of women. They seemed to be having a good time, and a couple of women from our group smiled at them and greeted them with the Turkish word for hello. They smiled back. None of them spoke English, nor were any of us fluent in Turkish. The next thing we knew, we were being offered tea and cakes. We asked if we could take some pictures, and the next 10 minutes were spent smiling at each other and into the camera lens. As we left, there were many hugs, and we felt a lasting impression of relatedness. It all started with smiling.

We can also feel acknowledged with a smile. When others are speaking, we let them know we are listening to them by nodding, making eye contact, and smiling. This encourages them to speak and makes them feel that they are valued and seen. Our smiles often let others know that it's safe to open up. In other situations, we may be involved in doing something that is difficult for us, and smiles encourage us on the way and greet us when we have completed the task.

This week, I read a newspaper story about a teacher training program in which the students were teachers learning how to teach other languages. The class was learning a number of languages, including Russian, Hebrew, and Arabic. There was a touchy moment when a Palestinian student and an Israeli student had an interaction; the class moved on, and yet this experience seemed to heighten everyone's sensitivities. Then, during a lesson in Hebrew, the teacher asked the Palestinian woman to say the word for orange in Hebrew. There was a pause; then she spoke the word, the teacher smiled, she smiled, and the Israeli woman smiled. Something had shifted. They found their connection through smiling.

One of the experiences that are offered at many interfaith gatherings is a simple form of dancing called The Universal Dances of Peace. They are done as a group, and there is interaction between everyone in the group as part of the dance. No words are spoken; one simply acknowledges the presence of the other with the eyes and perhaps a smile. There is an amazing sense of oneness and peace.

Once you begin to think about smiling as a part of listening, you will begin to notice many instances of the power of a smile to foster a more peaceful planet. There's a wonderful movie of two young boys, each from a culture that had been involved in fighting the other for decades. They met through a program that is designed to build bridges of peace. There was some tension when they first got together. Neither of them knew quite what to do. They played some competitive games that at first were serious—and then one of them smiled, then the other, then laughter, and then friendship.

A few years ago, I was in New York City with one of my daughters. We had heard all kinds of things about how people would be unfriendly and gruff and not to count on any help. What we discovered was that a friendly smile seemed to break through that reputation, and we found that people were extremely helpful, friendly, and kind to us. Our smiling impacted their listening to us.

Smiling transcends language. It is an invitation to participate, and often an irresistible one. There's a short movie about an incident in a New York subway. Somehow a bird's feather had found its way into one of the cars and landed on one man's head. A woman seated across from him noticed it and got his attention with a smile and some gestures; when he realized it was there, he blew air up toward the top of his head and launched the feather away. Then others in the car puffed on the feather as it came by them. Soon, several people were smiling and playing along. One smile and a feather connected a group of strangers for the moment; I suspect they all went away smiling to themselves about the wonder of that experience.

Smiling and listening—new ways of being together for a better world.

* * * * *

Kay Lindahl is the founder of The Listening Center in Laguna Niguel, California, and is recognized as an inspiring teacher and spiritual guide to people of all religious backgrounds.

☼

"Smiling is powerful, effective and scientifically based. Look in your mirror and try it!

"I have been practicing cosmetic dentistry for over 15 years now, and I can say without any hesitation that the smiles that result from my corrective surgery and dental enhancements transform the lives of my clients.

"The resulting beautiful smile I produce in my patients with corrective procedures brings happiness and a belief in themselves that they never had before.

"Your smile is your calling card."

—*Ohiro Yawamoto*
Cosmetic dentist and oral surgeon

Edgar Cayce on Smiling

In his hundreds of thousands of medical and spiritual readings for guidance, Edgar Cayce often mentioned the healing and joy-bringing power of the smile. Cayce helped President Roosevelt and tens of thousands of other famous names in Hollywood, politics, and the church, as well as medical doctors and psychologists, with help and career decisions.

The results he achieved are legendary.

Here are some of Cayce's smile reminders:

* * * * *

"Do smile under the strained conditions, the attempt to arise when possible, you gain that which would bring to self through smiling greater services as may be rendered to all. Do that."

* * * * *

"Your very smile, your very expression, gives the person the opportunity to ask for aid and help. Did you ever see anybody who had a frown on that you were willing to go up and speak anything to? What about how a smiling person makes you feel? Good, Yes?

"One of the things I think most of about the chiropractors is that their motto is 'Keep Smiling.' You know, when we look for light, we have to turn our face toward the sunlight. Smile and you can do more good than any other way."

* * * * *

"Smile and with the love as ye would have thy God show thee. Smile more every day and see the healing and strength it brings you and those you smile at."

* * * * *

"KEEP thy *smile* of encouragement to others; for it lightens the heart of many."

* * * * *

"For, as has been said, the smile raised hope in that one upon which it was given; that hope made possible activity; that activity made possible a haven for some discouraged, some disheartened soul! Be thou, each of you, one that may smile though the heavens fall; thou may SHINE even in Heaven if you can really Smile."

* * * * *

"Make thy life and thy love of thy fellow man a living thing in thine experience day by day. Smile oft. Always Smile as it heals and brings joy to you and all you Smile at."

* * * * *

"It is certainly true that when you smile the world smiles with you, when you weep you weep alone—that is, if you are weeping because of self-pity.

"Usually when we smile, REALLY smile, we are giving something of ourselves in joy and happiness to others. When we are self-pitying, complaining, blue, and discouraged, we are not only making ourselves miserable but we are adding destructive influences that are hard on all those who come in contact with us. Smile to create happiness; it heals everyone."

* * * * *

"Smile upon those that are downhearted and sad; lift the load from those that find theirs too heavy to bear, in gentleness, in kindness, in long-suffering, in patience, in mercy, in brotherly love. Your smile can bring happiness and recovery and renewed strength to those who give up. Be happy and glad. Smile though the heavens fall."

* * * * *

"Smile. Always Smile.

"So may one be joyous, being kind, being loving, being open-hearted, open-minded to those things wherein that in the word spoken, in the manifestation of the smile in the face, in the eye, to those that the self contacts, there is brought forth that from the hearts, the minds, the souls of those whom you contact day by day! Your Smile will heal."

* * * * *

"Smile and give courage to the disheartened, and STRENGTH comes from that as has been builded by the entity. But OVERCOME stress with GOOD, with deeds of kindness, a cheery word, a smile, a slap on the shoulder.

Smile!

An encouraging word and a genuine smile to the faltering gives strength not only to him who falters but aids SELF the more.

"Your Smile will help you and the person."

* * * * *

"Though ye may be spoken of harshly, smile—SMILE! For it is upon the river of Life that smiles are made."

☼

Smiling Increases Your Face Value

by Arthur H. Brownstein, M.D.

The study of smiling has been thoroughly researched as has the common sense, humor, and solid science behind the many reasons to smile daily.

Smile research needs to be on the coffee table of every home around the world, in every library, in every classroom, and on the bookshelves of every major academic center and university in the world, as well as in the personal offices of every professional in the world who deals with people, be they doctors, nurses, psychologists, counselors, educators, lawyers, public relations firms, human resource personnel, media personnel, (including TV and movie producers, journalists and reporters), and in the hands of just about everyone else interested in improving the quality of their life experience.

As a physician, I can't imagine a more effective or powerful prescription for health than the daily practice of smiling from the heart to increase your health and happiness.

* * * * *

Smile!

Arthur H. Brownstein, M.D., M.P.H., is an Assistant Clinical Professor of Medicine, John A. Burns School of Medicine, University of Hawaii at Manoa. Author of *Healing Back Pain Naturally* (Harbor Press, 1999) and *Extraordinary Healing* (Harbor Press, 2005).

☼

Smiling in the Courtroom

by Steve Slavit

"A smile can allow us to activate our higher reasoning centers for our own well-being."
—Steve Slavit

I have been a prosecutor with Los Angeles County for 19 years. During that time, I have tried approximately 16 murder cases. In my work, my activities and responsibilities include dealing with violent felons on a daily basis. I am currently prosecuting a defendant for killing a liquor store owner; we are seeking the death penalty.

Often, situations in the courtroom and at my office allow me to forget that the best method of dealing with any situation in life is to be able to draw from a great state of mind. I choose various lifestyle practices, such as hatha yoga and meditation, to stay in an optimum and resourceful state of mind. This state of mind is often contrary to the angry or fearful situations that seem to predominate. This is exactly why the technique of smiling is so important!

The experts state that the higher brain and emotional states are not present in the fear or anger states. We all make very bad decisions and statements when we are in the grip of dramas and cases like I see and hear in the courtroom. This is when we need to loosen the grip of the frowning, grimacing face. A smile can allow us to activate our higher reasoning centers for our own well-being.

The best result is one of "win-win," in which the real justice of balance becomes a reality through optimum thinking, feeling, and acting. A smile does just that: it assures those who see the smile that it is possible to respond to a tense proceeding with an open and resourceful attitude.

Note—I am writing this individually on my own behalf. This is only my view as a career prosecutor and is not necessarily reflective of the view of the Los Angeles District Attorney's Office.

* * * * *

Steve Slavit is a Prosecutor and L.A. County District Attorney

☼

Smiling in Sports

by Al McCoy
Sports Broadcaster for NBA,
Phoenix, Arizona

After I had broadcast NBA basketball for some 35 years, many things come to mind that certainly tie smiling into the world of competitive sports. As I turned the pages, it brought to mind the many unforgettable smiles of some of pro basketball's greatest players:

Sports Hall of Famer **Connie Hawkins** possessed a great "child-like" smile. **Dr. J. Julius Erving** had plenty to smile about. And how about the sensational smiles of such super stars as **Michael Jordan** and **Magic Johnson**. The thing I noticed with all of them is their smile.

Winners seem to smile more, and that is what makes them winners. Just thinking about great smiles, and you're thinking about so many great athletes. Thru the years I can't tell you how many of pro basketball's great coaches used "smiles" to encourage their players.

During time-outs after the x's and o's have been discussed, so many coaches send their players back on the floor with a smile and the phrase, "OK, let's go...and let's have some fun!"

A smile says: "We're on the same team." A smile says: "Let's create win-win...and let's do this together." Remember...WINNERS, SMILE!!!!!!

That's why they win.

☼

"I love to renew a person's smile in my dental practice. One can't help but smile and feel great when we see a good smile, no matter who is smiling.

"It makes us feel so happy to see a smile and it makes us happy to have one. A smiling face causes all to smile that see it and feel good.

"My clients are always overjoyed to see their new smile and they know that the rest of their lives they will have a fantastic greeting in their smile wherever they go.

"A smile from the heart is contagious. A smile can change a person's life."

—Dr. Paul Tanaka, DDS
Honolulu, Hawaii

213

Messages in Smiles

by Dr. Masaru Emoto

I travel around the world, and many people that I encounter ask me, "If you were to choose a place to live or to visit next, where would you like for it to be?"

Each time, I feel that it is not the place that makes it wonderful, but the smiling people that I meet in these places I visit.

The good energy and smiles that I receive from people are what I remember the most. When I think about all the people I have met, I wonder how many smiles I have encountered.

No matter how beautiful the land is, if there are no smiles, I do not want to go, and vice versa.

Smile and good HADO...this is what makes my work worthwhile, and I feel that I am contributing to a more peaceful world.

* * * * *

Dr. Masaru Emoto *is* the author of *The Hidden Messages in Water.*

☼

Smiling in Peace Negotiations

by Donald Fritts

In my career as a United Nations Command negotiator with North Korea and as the captain of a nuclear submarine in the Persian Gulf during *Operation Enduring Freedom* on the *USS Pasadena*, I have experienced some of life's most demanding and potentially stressful encounters.

The simple yet profound gesture of a human smile has the innate power to transform extremely stressful situations into more positive and rewarding experiences— even the ones like these.

The information and research and credible comments on smiling and its innate power are both scientific as well as humane. You will find smiling to be a most valuable resource for being genuinely happy in your life.

* * * * *

Donald Fritts is a U.S. Naval Commander, U.S. Navy, Ret., and a former United Nations peace negotiator

☼

Smiling in War:
The Creator of Peace

by Elan Sun Star

"Amidst the brutality of war in Iraq, the endless
attempts to feed starving children in Haiti,
the thankless separating of belligerents in
Bosnia and Kosovo, or providing humanitarian
assistance to Central America, the enduring
power of the human smile still spans the
barriers of culture, language and hatred."
—Christopher P. Hughes

Lt. Col. Chris Hughes, commander of the 2nd Battalion,
327th Infantry Regiment, was leading American forces
into the hometown of the Grand Ayatollah Ali Hussein
Sistani to seek his support in maintaining peace.

As they neared Sistani's home, a group of Iraqi civilians
blocked their way, shouting, "God is great!" in Arabic.
The crowd rapidly swelled. Many seemed to think that
the Americans were trying to capture the town's holy
man and attack the Imam Ali Mosque, a holy site for
Shiite Muslims around the world. The crowd started
throwing rocks at the troops.

Colonel Hughes showed restraint and intelligence, and
he used the power of the human smile to transform a
dangerous situation. He ordered his troops, "Smile!"

Then he commanded his soldiers to take a knee and point their weapons to the ground. Some Iraqis actually began smiling back, and some even patted the soldiers on the back.

Hughes then commanded his troops to walk away slowly backward while still smiling (and this was an order!). "Keep smiling and mean it."

The commander had to evaluate a dangerous situation and decide in a split second what action to take, and he had to know that his troops trusted him enough to obey. He had to know intuitively just the right gesture—the smile—that could speak the universal language of trust when none of the Iraqis spoke English and they were afraid that the battalion was there to take away their religious leader.

Though we are not taught to smile to avoid violent reactions in war, all humans know from history that the smile is the one gesture to rely on, no matter whom we are with or where in the world, in any culture. The smile is the one physical gesture in the world that means the same thing in any language.

This interpersonal skill has worked throughout history to save lives and create trust and cooperation, both in war and during peacetime.

Hughes was responsible for hundreds of soldiers, and he knew instinctively, without a second to think, that smiling had the power to defuse situations like this. Throughout history, the smile has been used for peace negotiations globally as well as in intense wartime situations. Obviously, only authentic smiles will work.

This gesture of respect (the smile) helped defuse a dangerous situation and made the Americans' peaceful intentions clear.

Ordering his troops to smile created an atmosphere that opened communications and prevented potential violence.

"In a world of technical solutions, converging societies, and globalization, there are still some truisms in humanity that cannot be 'spun' or misinterpreted, one of which is the warmth of the human smile," said Colonel Hughes. "I have witnessed the power of the human smile at the most basic levels of human endeavor for over 24 years in the United States Army. Smiling can change our planet."

* * * * *

Colonel Christopher P. Hughes is Commander, Joint Task Force Bravo, U.S. Army, Soto Cano Airbase, Honduras

☼

Part 3

Now It's Your Turn to Smile

Keep On Smiling

by Elan Sun Star

"What sunshine is to flowers, smiles are to humanity.
They are trifles, to be sure; but, scattered along life's
pathway, the good they do is inconceivable."
—*Joseph Addison*

The power of a smile is never-ending. Once you give a smile to others in your immediate physical environment, or even if you give the smile in a photograph, it spreads to everyone who comes in contact with it, and they go out feeling good and smiling, in turn affecting countless others. Thus, you can spread your smiles around the world, amplified by the millions, just by smiling or by sharing this book with others. You can remind them to surround the planet with smiles. Now, with the Internet, we can share the power of our smiles through digital photography and network our smiles around the world billions of times.

Would you like to share your smiling metaphors, quotes, anecdotal stories, or inspiring experiences? Let me know how a smile empowered you or a loved one, young or old. I'm looking forward to creating a world of smiling, hopeful people. Send your stories to me by e-mail, regular mail, or voice mail:

elansunstar@yahoo.com
Elan Sun Star
(808) 779-0073

What better purpose or mission than the sharing of smiles? It is so simple. It doesn't take planning or a board of directors or a large budget to make it happen. It's something you can do, and you can teach others to do it by doing it. And when you smile, your own heart keeps saying, "YES!" And your mind says, "YES!" And your body says, "YES!" And your spirit says, "YES!"

It keeps rebounding in an echo. Smiling is the best way to bring peace to the world—to say, "Let us forgive, let us live in the element of peaceful co-existence." Smiling reassures all that it is a safe world. Creating a smiling world seems like such a simple thing, and yet it can do so much.

Smiling can bring so much goodness, happiness, and joy to the world. As we realize that we're all in this together, by smiling we unleash heretofore hidden forces in our hearts, bodies, minds, and spirits. The research shows that smiling could be the most powerful thing you can do. To reveal that goodness is simple. A better world starts with a smile—nothing more.

The more you focus on that, the more you focus on the heart rather than on the problems, and the more you listen to the heart's arguments rather than those of the mind, the more you will be protected from negativity in the world. In other words, "Goodness is a radiance that casts no shadow."

Wherever you can bring a smile or stimulate one, you've brought healing, enrichment, and empowerment. On a crowded city street, in an elevator, in a checkout line, in the country, in your garden, in your home, while you're driving, while you're bathing, while you're talking, always make it a habit to smile. It's the best habit you could ever develop. It will automatically enhance your life so immeasurably that you'll come to realize that the best things in life are free. It will help nudge the other things in life into perspective.

Start making your dreams come true. Start with something that you can do right now. Smile! Throughout this book, I've given you helpful hints and research material. But do your own experiment. Give it a 30-day test and ask others around you to do the same, and find out what it can do for your life.

* * * * *

Program Yourself To Smile

Smile in a mirror at yourself, and you'll feel good all day long. If you smile at people around you, they'll love being around you, and they'll want to share their own smiles with others, too. If someone has a faint smile, help them to make it a big one.

You can use humor and laughter to cajole, and at the same time reinforce your own good feeling. Volumes could be written about the benefits of smiling, but let your own smile be your critical appraisal. Notice the feeling you get from it, and notice the responses of those around you.

Smiling is such a simple technique. Anywhere, anytime, smile. If you like, you can even e-mail your smiles and those of your loved ones. Big close-up smiles—lots of teeth, or no teeth! Get out your digital camera and send us your smiles so we can include them on our SMILING website and link you to others around the world who are part of the SMILING team. "Service with a smile" is our motto.

The inherent wholesomeness of a smile says the same thing, in the same language, to everyone it reaches, young or old. Goodwill and good intention create harmony in the world and within ourselves. As many of the researchers in this book have said, creating heart and brain coherence leads to a wholesome and happy life.

The best gift to give on a birthday or during the holidays is your smile. Include a smile with everything you do. When you're serving food, when you're walking along the street, when you're in line at the post office, keep smiling.

Allow yourself to remember all of the thousands of smiles you have received in your lifetime from family and friends, and from books and pictures. Let your memory roam. How did those smiles make you feel? Can you remember a smile that lifted you up when you were down, when someone special came into your life and smiled?

Beyond all the data, reference material, and personal experiences, a smile is the universal frequency that lifts your level of vibration to the highest spiritual practice. It allows you to be in a spiritual realm that transcends religions, dogmas, and differences. Use smiling as a spiritual practice, for it is nothing less.

A smile allows you to offset the challenges of the day. The higher frequency always cancels out the lower frequency. The higher power of love and joy prevails over fear, negativity, doubt, and shame, vibrating like a universal sun. Allow your smile to cover the whole world like the sun, and feel your smile warm your body like the warmth of the sun, thawing out the chill of winter. Smile in truth from your heart. A smile is the greatest gift we can give each other.

KEEP SHINING AND KEEP SMILING!

A Peaceful World Begins With Our Feelings

by Elan Sun Star

In today's world, there's a whole litany of excuses as to why we can't smile.

There's no reason to smile.

Or things are too rough to smile.

Or we only smile when we're happy, when we are already effervescent, when we are feeling exuberance and joy.

If we learn to let go of what we perceive as problems and live as if we were already manifesting that which we desire, we will find it easier to smile. Begin with the end in mind, and live life's ideal reality.

Smiling is part of that reality. Smiling expresses many states of mind—contentment, happiness, joy, love, acceptance, gratitude, appreciation, and many, many others that are expressions of the ideal world.

But a smile is not limited to any one emotional state or expression. If we start with a smile, we can create a full slate of desirable states of mind, feelings, and emotions.

Consumerism, doubt, lack, and fear are so prevalent in today's society that it takes discipline to remember to smile regardless of the external circumstances.

Earlier in this book, we said that you should smile first, rather than waiting for a reason to smile.

Did that feel strange to you? Did it make you feel like you were trying to be manipulative? Do you still stubbornly refuse to smile unless you have a reason? Or can you see that smiling is a desirable end in itself, one that you can choose to create? All it takes is moving a few facial muscles and a willingness to let your mind, body, and spirit grow into a real smile.

The emotions that you desire, you can create with a smile. When you want a glass full of water, you have to start by pouring a little bit of water into a glass. So, if you want a state of happiness, joy, contentment, appreciation, gratitude, love, and harmony, start with a smile. That is the equivalent of putting the first few drops of water into your glass.

There is a recurring theme throughout this book. Smiling is an integral part of all relationships, whether they are personal or corporate, whether they take place in the office or across a negotiating table.

Smiling is an integral part of owning up to the desired outcome. So start with the desired state (smiling) and work your way backwards to changing the dynamics of the situation. Let the smile change your biochemistry, and it will ultimately result in a change in the relationship. Any relationship.

* * * * *

Smile for World Peace

Many individuals feel overwhelmed and disempowered when it comes to their ability to bring about global change. International peace, ending war, preventing hostile and critical factions from influencing world politics…what can a single person do in the face of such overwhelming odds? And yet, it is in this one area that the simple smile can possibly have its greatest impact.

It seems astounding that so few peace negotiators, winners of the Nobel Peace Prize, or members of the Nobel Committee itself have attempted to demonstrate that something so simple as a smile can be effective. They always want to negotiate from a position of strength—and yet I am advocating that you instead bring about peace from a position of humility. I entreat all of you to use your personal—and sublime—power to dramatically alter the balance of global peace efforts. Create harmony in political situations as well as in personal situations. Bring peace and abundance to every situation, for all of humanity, no matter where in the world.

Encourage clear proliferation—of smiles. Let them proliferate in yourself, in your family, and in your local community, and continue the proliferation through travel and tourism, through the Internet, and through images in the press, whether in a tabloid, a magazine, television, or the movies. Help bring about an exponential increase

in happy, loving, caring smiles. Help make smiling the norm in life, not the exception.

If we assume there's a problem in the world and deny ourselves the glorious beauty of experiencing happiness, joy, and peace right now, we unknowingly and unwittingly allow the situation of non-peace to exist in the world and in our communities. But by using that most simple yet powerful tool, the smile, we can find a way to create peace in the world now. NOW is a good time for peace.

I saved the chapter on global peace negotiations for the end of this book because I feared it would need the most bibliographical proof. And yet, on reflection, I am pleased to see that

global peace is the outcome of the combined benefits of smiling.

We are conditioned to believe that the powers and principalities of the world dictate global economics, international relationships, and even war and peace. By doing so, we deny ourselves the very power which was given to us from the beginning. Each of us has the innate ability to express the divinity that created us. This is not an ecclesiastical statement; it is simply a statement of fact.

You are a hologram of the universe. Anything that you participate in, be it biochemically, physiologically, emotionally, psychologically, or consciously, is what you proliferate. That is what you are giving your vote to.

To give your vote for peace, smile to yourself, smile to your friends, and smile to your community, your family, and the world. That is the way to bring about world peace. Where there is a smiling community and a smiling world, there will never be a war again. War is the ultimate expression of a frown.

The peace "experts" of our society, whether they be Nobel Peace Prize winners or members of the Nobel committee, do not need to dictate to us who they think is bringing about peace. We can take back our power with our smiles and say, "We determine the state of the world."

The irony has been pointed out before. Nobel gained his fortune in large part due to gunpowder and dynamite. The ability to establish the Nobel prizes came in large part from the munitions of war—not necessarily the purest source for seeding a peaceful world. In the end, it will be our choice to create world peace, not through munitions, but through the simple expression of smiling.

We have "the cart before the horse," as the old phrase goes. We honor individuals and agencies—for example, the United Nations, the Nobel Peace laureates—for telling us what we can and cannot do to create a better world, acting on the assumption that the simple things we can do are either out of our hands or beyond our comprehension.

We create the world through our beliefs. We can, through our subjective reality, research the feelings that smiling brings to our bodies, minds, and spirits. We can then help spread those feelings around the world, creating in each person the foundation of a peaceful world.

Start with the end in mind: peace, happiness, joy, and contentment. Expand it to the world, and you have global peace.

World peace is the ultimate result of spreading the "smiling virus."

 We're conditioned to believe that simple solutions are not effective. That is one of the dilemmas we face in today's world. But in a world filled with negativity, the simple approach may be the best approach. Smiling is ubiquitous. It is a universal language that is effective at bringing about a state of mental, physical, and emotional well-being in individuals. By projection, if we spread a smile broadly enough, we will achieve global well-being.

We can create a world of peace, not by hoping and wishing and singing and imagining, but by doing.

It is not esoteric; it is not metaphysical; it is not difficult. It is so simple that we have difficulty accepting it, for no other reason than its sheer simplicity.

One simple way to propagate peace is by forming "smiling societies." Share smiles through Internet groups, for example. Network with "laughter clubs" around the world. Do networking in your own community. With enough participants, smiling can gain its proper, powerful, and exuberant dominion.

Smiling is instinctive. The impulse to smile is inherent in every individual. And yet, through cultural conditioning, mostly imposed by the advertising media, we have been taught to be dissatisfied. We have learned to frown instead of smile.

Yes, indeed. As a photographer, I have seen my photos used in tens of thousands of ads, commercials, and layouts.

I quickly realized that the reason smiling faces are used so much in advertising is because Madison Avenue wants to associate products with happiness and satisfaction, which are desirable states.

Hence, smiles have been associated with everything from real estate to liquor, from tobacco to violence.

Why violence? Because the fear, doubt, and worry elicited by violence convert people who were quite happy with their lot into people looking for psychological security, and they are told they can acquire that security by purchasing a product. They are hoping to regain the inherent happiness they had before they were scared out of their wits.

Over the millennia, the smile has been given an exalted place in medicine. You can find the smile playing an important role in traditional Chinese medicine, in Ayurvedic medicine, in ancient Greek medicine, and even in modern Western medicine (*e.g.*, Patch Adams). Court jesters were kept close to the king to keep him smiling. Smiling prevents disease, and in some cases even cures illness.

So why isn't this taught to everyone when they go to the doctor's office? The reason is all too obvious. Those who have something to sell us, whether they are pharmaceutical companies or automobile manufacturers, make money from our problems and worries.

The results that sell people on a product are happiness, joy, and contentment. Smiling represents all of these. If you already have smiling and joy, you don't need to purchase products.

* * * * *

Look around your environment. The people you're most attracted to are the smiling people, the happy people. They seem to be the most attractive, no matter how they appear physically. The same goes for you. Your own attractiveness is dramatically enhanced by smiling.

Thus, smiling is a sizeable portion of that which we want to create, for most of us. If you envision a happy you, a happy relationship, a good job, or a peaceful world, the first part of the visualization is to make it tangible. And the simplest tangible sign of happiness is the smile.

For every element I've included in *Smile!*, there are thousands of others I left out. I purposely ignored a lot of my research on smiling and wrote from the heart.

When I interviewed people for *Smile!*, I invited them to participate and share their own contemporary research and experience, along with anecdotal stories about smiling. But I did not want to make this a book of quotes referencing other people's material and research. The few references in the book are used primarily as illustrations. The best material is still being generated right now, and it will evolve as we co-create a smiling world.

Smiling is so simple that it is beyond needing proof. Unfortunately, we have been conditioned to believe that the most highly evolved principles are those that are complex and difficult to know.

We have been conditioned to think that that which is childlike is childish. Yet nothing could be farther from the truth. That which is most important to the quality of life, and to life itself, is the common, ubiquitous smile. It is necessary every moment of the day, not once in a while. Smiling is like breathing. It has to be there in order to live…to truly live.

Energy and life itself are attracted to smiling and put off by frowning. In other words, smiling increases the ability to attract energy and life force. It is a magnetic participation in life itself.

You may be asking why such a simple and obvious procedure as smiling needed a whole book to explain and prove its importance. The answer: it doesn't. What does need the effort is overcoming the conditioning that says something simple cannot possibly be that important.

We accept breathing as a metaphor for living, and it's pretty obvious what happens when we don't breathe. Try doing this experiment right now.

Don't breathe for five minutes and see how you feel.

Report back after five minutes.

Now, if you've managed not to breathe for five minutes, try it for 15 minutes and report back.

If you've managed to stop breathing for 15 minutes, I will assume that you'll be listed on tomorrow's obituary page.

Okay. Experiment over.

It's so important to breathe that you can only go for a short period without doing it. And yet, in today's world, shallow breathing is probably one of the major causes of disease. We can probably do without 99% of the things we think of as necessary to life, but breathing is absolutely essential.

Likewise, we don't realize how important smiling is. That which is ubiquitous is too often taken for granted. We want wealth—material goods. The more things we have, the stronger and more powerful we are. But that is the lie of the age. If we learn this, we will move a long way toward regaining our original state of happiness and joy.

The proof is in the pudding. Without any documentation, without theories to back things up, we can prove to ourselves that smiling makes us feel good. Smiling makes our hearts feel good and our spirits feel good.

Smiling makes those around us feel good. Smiling makes our communities work better. It makes the world harmonious and cooperative. Smiling can actually be a driving force for world peace, as simplistic as that sounds.

There will never be 100% agreement on what is important in life. People's view of Reality is subjective. Regardless of where you stand, however, you cannot help but agree that smiling makes you feel good, or that you smile when you do feel good. We can smile and we can feel good in spite of the opinions of any naysayers.

It has been the goal throughout this book to lay a foundation by stating simply, without the need for proof, without validation by outside authorities, that smiling can create world peace. Amazing!

It is a testimony to the potency of smiling that no proof is needed. Smiling is world peace because it is inner peace, familial peace, community peace, national peace, and, by extension, world peace.

If you have supporting research material to offer, if you are part of an organization that is working toward the goal of peace, or if you wish to contribute your vote for world peace, share your comments, letters, and anecdotes about smiling for world peace and/or personal peace with us via the *Smile!* website, e-mail, or post. *Smile!* is not just a book: it is an ongoing evolution of material stimulated by this book. Sharing our vision of a smiling world makes it easier to achieve.

Your feedback, your stories, and your lifetime network are the most important parts of *Smile!*. This book is nothing more than a beginning. You may be used to finishing a book and then putting it down and forgetting it, but that will not happen in this case. The subject of smiling will continue to resonate throughout your lifetime. Help amplify that resonance.

Nothing has been accomplished until we create a new, peaceful world. Global peace does not start with forcing others to accept our political views or concepts—it comes with allowing peace to be. A big part of that is allowing smiling to settle into the core of your being and allowing it to radiate into the world. Smiling spreads the peace virus, which is contagious. It is neither a philosophy, nor a dogma, nor a religion. Peace is a state of allowing peace.

Smiling allows the space for this to happen, beginning with your own self.

It is in peace that I leave you with the final words of this book.

The future history of the world will be created by you. Peace cannot be won with bombs and guns, nor can it be won with philosophies and dogmas. Peace cannot be created through psychological operations (psyops), through therapy, or through more books on the subject. Peace is up to you. Smile. Spread the smiling virus and contribute to world peace. The secret is in spreading it around the world. Use images, work your networks, and smile in public to everyone you meet.

The challenge is an enjoyable one. It will bring you happiness and joy. How can you possibly turn down this challenge?

Smile.

Be peace.

Start with the end in mind: the most incredible life you can imagine. When you visualize yourself enjoying your passion, remember that in that vision, you're always smiling. Remember it deeply.

Start with the end in mind. Smile. And rather than saying this is the end, say this is just the beginning.

☼

Postscript

We do not have to prove how important a baby's smile is—we can see the contentment and joy that it expresses. Likewise, we do not have to be told that smiling is world peace. We can already see that smiling brings personal peacefulness, abundance, and fulfillment. Expand the thought to an ever wider circle, and you have world peace.

We've already filled a whole book with proof and research. We have enough evidence! That which is obvious does not really need any proof. It is much too simple.

One area of concern arises with situations in which smiling seems to be counter-productive—for example, in the corporate environment. Every country worries about the gross national product. In everyday terms, they are talking about agricultural production, manufacturing, services, and so forth: the "stuff" of the business world.

Throughout this book, we've talked about another product that is an end in itself: the smile. When we visualize an end goal that makes us happy, we smile. Our happiness represents the end already having been fulfilled. So, let's start with the end in mind.

The advertisers would have us assume that the only reason corporations exist is to create more things that will make us happy, so we can smile more. So start with the end.

Smile first and work your way backwards. For example, if you are building a jigsaw puzzle, it is helpful to know the picture that the puzzle composes. It helps to put the pieces into the right perspective.

If we don't start with the smile first and work our way backwards, how can we piece together a picture of what we want to achieve? We have to start with the whole picture—with contentment, abundance, and prosperity. We have to know what economic result we want and what will make us happy. From there, we can begin to fill in the pieces.

How can this visualized abundance bring us anything? Go back to the original question. How can the jigsaw puzzle be put together if you can't see the picture of what the puzzle is?

When you get a jigsaw puzzle, the cover of the box shows you what the completed puzzle will look like, no matter whether it's a puzzle of ten thousand pieces or one hundred pieces. We have one goal in mind: the final picture and how all the pieces fit. But before we even buy the puzzle, we have to see the picture.

Let's get the picture of what we want first. We want to begin with a smile and work our way back to where we are right now.

From there, ask yourself the question, "What does smiling mean to me?" Contentment? Peace? Fulfillment, abundance, prosperity? Great relationships? World peace? Family peace, joy, happiness? Whatever smiling means to you, act as if you have it now._

This "act as if you already have that state of happiness" technique will create that happiness in your subconscious mind. *Smile right now,* regardless of whether you feel you have the thing or the feeling you want. Smiling reinforces the feeling you want to cultivate.

Without the smile, how can you have joy or happiness? How can you have prosperity or great relationships that you don't have now? Start with the smile; end with the smile.

Start with the smile, just as you would start with the picture of the jigsaw puzzle. Once you have the picture in mind, you can begin to sort out the pieces and figure out how they fit together to form the completed picture.

Don't try to create corporate economic productivity and success unless you start with a smile. Have the goal of happiness before you start. Don't hope to bring about global peace, or even cooperation within your own family, without first visualizing happy results and starting with a smile. Start with the picture of the jigsaw puzzle, and then figure out how to put all of those puzzle pieces together to create the picture in reality.

No matter what you want in your life, smiling will get you there faster, especially if the smile is an integral part of the state you are trying to achieve.

What human being would say that he or she does not want to smile? Probably not somebody you'd want to know. Happiness should be part of the goal, so no matter what your goal is, start with the completed picture. Start with the outcome.

Most people are in a cultural trance that has been reinforced since time immemorial. The trance says that we don't know, that there is some "expert" who knows the answers that are too complicated for us. The "expert," if you but knew, lives inside of you. Listen to that expert. Find the state of being that you want to accomplish, and be in that state. Go directly to that state. Feel it. Let it make you happy. Feel it to your core. There is no better time to start than right now. If you are in the now, and you deeply feel that state of happiness that brings a smile to your face, then you already know the joy, abundance, prosperity, and peace that you want to accomplish. Begin with a smile, and you already know how to create the end result.

How? If economic strategies and peace negotiations were working, we'd all be very happy about the state of the world, and we would be doing well financially. The old ways aren't working. They need to be abandoned.

So what does work? To find out, picture yourself living in the best of all possible worlds for yourself. In this picture, you can be with whomever you want, wherever you want, being the person you want to be. Now, in that picture, look at your face. Do you have a smile or a frown? Hopefully, you have a smile. If not, start over again and work harder on imagining your ideal world.

There you have your answer. Start with a smile, and the rest will follow. It doesn't work the other way around.

If we try to get what we want by following the teachings or guidance of outside authorities, no matter how brilliant and generous they may be, we are denying our own inner authority. That is the real danger of listening to any voice outside your own heart and soul.

You already know the good feeling when you smile, but the cultural trance many people are in says that life is supposed to be difficult. That is the whole danger of accepting a false philosophy: you ignore the simple truth, the good feeling that comes from a simple smile.

The smile is not only simple, it's free. And it's right there for the taking. You don't even need a reason to smile. Just smile, and that will create the reason.

Try it. It may take a while to get over the conditioning, but keep trying. Those facial muscles may be stiff and hard. In Chinese philosophy and in the philosophy of Western thinkers such as Henry David Thoreau, anything that is living is flexible, moist, and growing. Things that are dry and brittle are dying or dead, and lack lifeforce. By becoming flexible, you take on the characteristics of a living thing. Drop old belief systems, drop the cultural conditioning, and embrace that which is living and growing. Embrace life!

The leading causes of death in our modern world are not heart disease and cancer, but frowning and, as the joke goes, "hardening of the attitudes."

Remember to smile. Remember, the stakes are high. You are smiling for nothing less than a new world of peace, both inner and outer. Your smile will spread around the world in a powerful explosion of caring and goodness.

Put this book down now and smile. Look at your reflection in a mirror. What you see in the mirror is what is reflected to the world at large: make sure it's a smile. Your smile is the key to everything.

www.sunstarphotography.com

Elan Sun Star

More Exciting books from **Peter Ragnar** and **ROARING LION PUBLISHING**
800-491-7141 — RoaringLionPublishing.com

Peter Ragnar

Since 1984, **Roaring Lion Publishing** has been committed to publishing best selling books and other products designed to inspire and tap into our human potential.

We now have a vast worldwide distribution, which continues to grow daily. We also wanted give our friends and clients the ability to secure their financial future by acquiring precious metals by investing in **Golden Lion Mint.** You can find out more by going to **GoldenLionMint.com.**

The Awesome Science of Luck

I WON, I WON!!!

I just finished Peters new book, *The Awesome Science of Luck* on Saturday. Saturday night, I went to a benefit and won a DVD player. The very next day I went to another benefit and won a 50/50 raffle. On both wins I had decided to give away the prize before I won. So each time I was detached as to whether I would win or not. This is by far my favorite Peter book.

J. Fradette—Cleveland, OH

How would you like to have the formula for the potent seeds you can plant in your mind that make "good luck" your way of life?

Actually, you'll discover that the incredible power of luck is a science. I know you may think this is unbelievable, but it's true—you can learn how to win with mind-boggling consistency. When would you like to start cashing in?

The Luminous Life

The Luminous Life was written to depict heroes as they should be...mentors to emulate. The heroes from this delightful and engaging story would be considered as strange as men from Saturn in the present world of the wimp. They are not ingratiating cowards or compromising phonies. They are rational lovers of truth. They are as bold, forthright, and virtuous as they are kind, warm, and tender. I hope this book gives you the encouragement to stretch and reach for your highest self. May you break down all the prison walls of limitation. May you fly into the light of the Luminous Life!

How Long Do You Choose to Live?

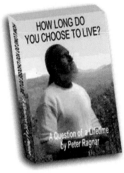

"ROLLING DICE WITH YOUR HEALTH WILL KILL YOU...

How would you like to improve your odds? You'd love to have the deck stacked in your favor, wouldn't' you?"

"What if you could override previous ideas about health, aging, athletic performance, and death?"

Imagine... if you could live to be 100 with the same youthfulness you had when you were 18, you'd be thrilled, wouldn't you? What if I said to 120 years (many scientists wonder why that limit isn't tested more) that would be even better, wouldn't it?

There is not a shred of scientific evidence to prove you cannot reverse aging, attain vibrant health and youthful levels of athletic performance at any age. In my book *How Long Do You Choose To Live?*, you'll find an abundance of examples. I'm certain you'll love to share in my discoveries and have your eyes opened to a whole new world of possibilities.

Wisdom of the Mystic Mountain Warrior

Edward Armstrong shares compelling insights from his weekly jujitsu lessons with his teacher and modern-day sage, Peter Ragnar. *Wisdom of the Mystic Mountain Warrior: Life Lessons from a Master of the Mixed Martial Arts*, is a delightful reference book for the soul, chockfull of Peter's revolutionary methods and techniques for success on and off the mat. Pursuit of excellence and high-voltage integrity create the foundation for the secrets of success revealed in the book.

Learn more about how Peter slays the dragons of self-doubt that have prevented so many from believing in their own capabilities. *Wisdom of the Mystic Mountain Warrior* reveals how Peter gives a polite nod to all things dark and scary and simply proceeds to live a fully committed life with a boldness that is nothing less than heroic.

---

10 Steps to a Magnetic Personality DVD (with FREE Bonus CD)

Do you know some people who appear to live a charmed life? That special person who everybody seems to love? The one who always seems to be getting the lucky breaks in life? On the other hand, do you know some people with negative charisma and just seem to repel the good things they say they desire? This is the kind of person that always seems to be rubbing you the wrong way.

What makes the difference between these two people? One applies the universal law of good fortune. The other simply does not to their own misfortune. The difference between struggling through life and making life a success is so simple. Today you can develop a magnetic personality in Ten Easy Steps, and attract all the things you want into your life.

The Art and Science of Physical Invincibility

 A nine-year-old boy playing on a construction site had an 1800-pound cast iron pipe roll onto him. As he struggled in the sand, a passerby who was a 56-year-old heart patient ran up and lifted the pipe off the boy's head. By the way, how's your dead lift? Amazing and true accounts of superhuman strength performed by ordinary people. You've got to be wondering as I once did, "How can I tap into the source of such power?" Oddly, the creation of such a mighty force does not require bulging muscles. If you will for a moment, consider a fire hose?" When not in use, it is soft and pliable, but when water is flowing through it, not even the strongest of men can bend it. Actually, the body itself has this same power. Now you can learn how to channel your energy in this same way to create amazing feats of strength.

For the first time, these secrets are revealed in this step-by-step, easy to understand program. *The Art and Science of Physical Invincibility* will at last disclose how you can transform yourself from a mortal, disease-prone human into a super-being!

Success Seekers Guide to the Opulent Reality

 Almost all of us have been programmed by classical conditioning to resent the wealthy on a subconscious level. Now tell me—how can you become financially independent if you secretly or unknowingly hold resentment? This anti-opulence programming is so deceptive and insidious most people never even know or suspect they have it.

How can you tell if you have this disease?

First: By how hard you have to work for money.

Second: By the subconscious resistance you create to receive it.

The opulent reality is eager to shower great prosperity upon you. But why is it so difficult to be a receiver? Why do you make mistakes with money? It's all because the subconscious brakes have been locked. Once you release them, you'll be utterly amazed at how much financial horsepower you already have in your internal wealth machine. You can just step on the gas and power poles will go by like a picket fence. Do you want this kind of power?

Rare Interviews

*"I've had countless world famous natural health practitioners on my program. But folks, I've got to say it—no one holds a light to **Peter Ragnar!** He is by far the most exciting and controversial guest I've ever had."*

Bob McCauley: Author, lecturer, syndicated radio talk show celebrity. *Lansing, MI*

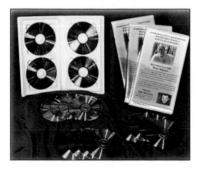

"The Rare Interviews with Peter Ragnar is a virtual banquet of ideas—ideas you can actually use."

You'll never be left alone in the dark when your health is at stake!

That is, not if you have these mind-stunning health revelations that I've packaged in an audio collection you'll want to listen to over and over again. And as you do, you'll not only find yourself effortlessly becoming an expert in health and natural healing, but in the process develop a vigorous, healthy body as living proof!

"Armed with this information, imagine you can operate at peak performance every day, and also help those you love to achieve that as well."

Your partner in achieving radiant health,
Peter

Quest for Excellence DVD

Will you invite me into your home?
My special reason for wanting to spend time with you is to share ideas that my friends confess have greatly helped them in the quest for human excellence.
How important is it for you to stay inspired, motivated and productive? Good! Then you're going to really appreciate what this One Hour DVD will be able to do for you..

Seven Secrets

SEVEN SECRETS TO THE FOUNTAIN OF YOUTH THAT ANYONE CAN APPLY IN SEVEN MINUTES OR LESS!

Can I share with you Seven Simple Secrets?

These secrets can be done in as little time as seven minutes a day! Are you ready to produce miracles in your life? When might be the best time to get started? This 80 Minute Audio CD reveals simple steps you can take to become more youthful and vibrant regardless of your age.

SEVEN Secrets to the Fountain of Youth that anyone can Apply in Seven Minutes or Less!
By Peter Ragnar

Unveiled Mystery of Self Mastery

"Are you Sick and Tired of Having Your Strings Pulled by an Invisible Puppeteer?"

Do emotional arguments with those you love leave you feeling drained and discouraged? Does intimidation from your employer, local bureaucracies, in-laws, or others make you feel frustrated and defenseless? Certainly you'd agree that taking complete charge of your own life would reward you with unbelievable confidence and courage.

"Yes, now with the step-bystep guidance you'll receive in the ***Unveiled Mystery of Self-Mastery*** course, you'll uncover a treasure chest of inner wealth!"

You'll own the real secret to mind power!

ROARING LION

800-491-7141   •   RoaringLionPublishing.com